@TechnicallyRon's
LIFE-ABET
An A to Z of Existence

D0293918

Aaron Gillies

BLINK
bringing you closer

Published by Blink Publishing

107–109 The Plaza
535 King's Road
Chelsea Harbour
London
SW10 0SZ

www.blinkpublishing.co.uk
facebook.com/blinkpublishing
twitter.com/blinkpublishing

978-1-910536-24-7

Typography by Steve Leard — LEARD.CO.UK

Printed and bound in Lithuania
1 3 5 7 9 10 8 6 4 2

Papers used by Blink Publishing are natural, recyclable products made from wood grown in sustainable forests. The manufacturing processes conform to the environmental regulations of the country of origin.

Every reasonable effort has been made to trace copyright holders of material reproduced in this book, but if any have been inadvertently overlooked the publishers would be glad to hear from them.

Blink Publishing is an imprint of the Bonnier Publishing Group
www.bonnierpublishing.co.uk

THIS BOOK IS DEDICATED TO:

My wife Lex, to whom I owe everything
My parents, for creating something so awesome and being
awesome themselves
My brother Cal, who occasionally shows up
Anna Kendrick because reasons
The Academy
The staff of Blink Publishing
Becky Thomas (my agent who did all the work)
James Walmsley for his amazing illustrations
Emily and Oli from Blink Publishing for putting up with me
My friends who don't hate me
Those who follow me on Twitter
Everyone that booed George Osborne at the 2012 Paralympics
All dogs everywhere
That guy in the coffee shop in Kentish Town who knows my order
Dobby the House Elf (RIP)
T-Pain
Mrs Rhodes from sixth-form English who said I wouldn't amount to anything
Dwayne The Rock Johnson for his continued support
The staff of The Barrels Public House In Hereford, UK
Tim Berners-Lee
Your mum

CONTENTS

AARON GILLIES

(Pronoun) Idiot.

This is me

25% neuroses

45% social awkwardness

30% legs

Good morning, didn't see you there. Welcome to this book. As you spent your hard-earned money on this tree corpse I have packed with words, I will attempt to make it worth your while. Unless you haven't got anything on at the moment, in which case make yourself a cup of tea (DON'T PUT THE MILK IN FIRST, YOU SAVAGE!) and settle down for a bit.

You may know me through my twitter name @TechnicallyRon. If you do recognise me from that name I apologise immensely. I enjoy pictures of dogs making friends with animals they wouldn't normally make friends with, public houses and long walks on the beach. Actually, the long walks on the beach thing is bollocks. Have you ever been for a long walk on a beach? This is Britain, a long walk on the beach means wind being bloody everywhere and sand in folds of your body you wish you didn't have.

I started using Twitter as a rather fantastic escape from my socially awkward lifestyle. After being diagnosed with mental health issues, namely depression, I used Twitter as a pub. I knew the people there, I made a dick of myself most of the time and met a girl. I think that's what the internet is for.

I discovered, much to my surprise, that I could make people laugh, mainly attractive people in all fairness. Yeah, I mean you. I say make them laugh, words I hurled at them apparently made people smile, and so after many years of doing very little with my life, I found out I wasn't utterly crap at something.

What follows this introduction is a definition of the subjects that we all face in our everyday lives. This is a self-help book for people who don't need help. A guide for people who don't need guidance. An A–Z of modern life.

If you are enjoying this book, try one of the many autobiographies I have written over the years:

OTHER TITLES FROM THIS AUTHOR

How to fuck up a perfectly normal situation just by turning up
Self-help book
I ate too much and now I feel sick, yet I regret nothing
Children's book
I am sorry I chased your dog for two miles
Court ordered autobiography
Existential crisis #67
Graphic novel
Drinking coffee to avoid social situations
An erotic novella
That one time I did exercise and ended up in A&E
Children's book (highly unpopular)

Anyway, thank you and I hope you enjoy the 104 little rants in this book. If you agree with any of the points, please feel free to buy me a drink. If you are affected by any of the issues raised in the book, there is no helpline, maybe the Samaritans. Or babestation.

P.S no refunds.

ADVERTS

*Ways to control your mind and slowly
ingest you into the capitalist machine*
WHAT DO YOU MEAN, I AM PARANOID?

How often, when you are sat at work, or at home, do you get a really fucking annoying theme tune stuck in your head? You can be slumped there, one hand on a keyboard, the other scratching your head, and a song about car insurance, or yoghurt, or hoovers is stuck on the brain.

Advertising has grown as humanity has grown. From the early televised adverts of young happy families enjoying a bassoon or something, to the 1980s trope of a father disappointing his family with gravy, to the modern day, where young women dance in black and white hotel rooms and discuss periods over a Diet Coke. This forced capitalism controls so many aspects of our lives. Our clothes have labels across the front of them, turning us into walking advertisements. Our phones leave a 'sent from my...' on every status or email. Our headphones have giant B's on the side of them for BELLEND and so forth.

The big question, however, is WHY DO WOMEN LOVE YOGHURT SO MUCH?!

Yeah, she's happy   **This just looks suspicious**   **The fuck are you laughing at?**   **This woman is apparently having a stroke**

To find out, I asked several women eating yoghurt in a well-known café chain, and their responses varied from 'Please go away' to 'Who are you?'. So, this will remain one of life's unanswered mysteries.

Like a creepy uncle at a birthday party, advertising follows you everywhere. However much you try to avoid adverts, they keep appearing behind you, tapping you on the shoulder and humming, until you turn around.

And they're devious. BuzzFeed will run an article entitled '33 BEYONCE GIFS THAT SUMMARISE STALINISM' and it's only when you get to the end that you realise it has been sponsored by KitKat or Durex. Likewise, before you can enjoy that YouTube video of a hippo farting you have to sit through three adverts first.

And then there are the clickbait ads, the ones that claim 'THIS MAN MAKES £300 A MINUTE SNIFFING CHEESE ONLINE' or 'THIS NEW DIET WILL MAKE YOU LOOK LIKE A COATRACK COVERED IN HAM IN ONLY TWO WEEKS!' Just as you quite reasonably try and run away, or look at porn, a bloody pop-up appears of a computer pretending to be a woman saying she is three metres away from you, which in any situation would be terrifying. I don't want a hot single in my AREA. Why do they want me?

Adverts just want you to feel like you have a shit life and are unattractive. 'ARE YOU BEACH BODY READY?' asks one brand on a poster featuring a woman who has just eaten a gym. As much as you want to say 'YES, I AM FUCKING BEACH BODY READY' and 'I LOVE WOBBLING LIKE A BLANCMANGE IN A TURBINE' and 'NO, I DON'T WANT TO SHARE A COKE WITH CAROL, CAROL CAN FUCK OFF' you can't help feeling like there is something wrong with the way you are right now. 'HAVE YOU BEEN INJURED AT WORK?' Yes, most days actually, in one way or another, but that's life, mate. I don't really need compensating for jabbing my leg on the corner of that desk, that is just wrong. Or is it?

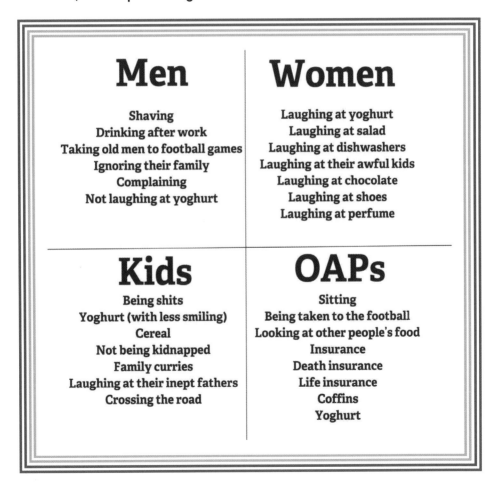

Men

Shaving
Drinking after work
Taking old men to football games
Ignoring their family
Complaining
Not laughing at yoghurt

Women

Laughing at yoghurt
Laughing at salad
Laughing at dishwashers
Laughing at their awful kids
Laughing at chocolate
Laughing at shoes
Laughing at perfume

Kids

Being shits
Yoghurt (with less smiling)
Cereal
Not being kidnapped
Family curries
Laughing at their inept fathers
Crossing the road

OAPs

Sitting
Being taken to the football
Looking at other people's food
Insurance
Death insurance
Life insurance
Coffins
Yoghurt

As my last note on the subject, I would like to make my idea for the new John Lewis Christmas advert known:

IDEA #452 For The John Lewis Christmas Ad:

[Camera pans down over a snowy countryside, a ukelele version of a popular song plays in the background. [Possibly smack my bitch up]]

David Cameron shoots a badger

turn to camera

'You can't afford Christmas'
end

ANXIETY

*When you want your brain to be in Helvetica
but it insists on converting everything to
CAPITALISED WORDART WITH WEIRD
DROPSHADOWS AND STUFF.*

Anxiety ranges from mild to severe. Mild is worrying that you've missed the last train, severe is worrying that you will die because you dropped a mug. My first proper anxiety attack occurred when I dropped a mug while I was washing up. I thought I was having a heart attack. My chest felt compressed, my brain felt like a collapsed beach ball. I breathed like an asthmatic rhinoceros. Since then, I have experienced many frightening responses to normally harmless events. I have arrived at the conclusion that my brain is a complete idiot.

Brain: This seems like a normal situation, doesn't it?
Me: Yeah...?
Brain: Would be a shame if...
Me: No
Brain: YOU RUINED EVERYTHING
Me: For the sake of fuck

Anxiety often comes hand in hand with depression. What would feeling awful about everything be without being hysterical about everything too. Mental health issues like to couple up, like a new couple at a dinner party, holding onto each other, ignoring everyone else, so that when one chemical imbalance mates with another, your other emotions just feel alienated and slightly disgusted.

When you feel like you are about to go crazy, count to four on your fingers. Place the tip of your index finger on the tip of your thumb, then your middle finger on your thumb, then your ring finger on your pinkie. Do this slowly and then count to four as you move along your fingers. Inhale as you count down, then exhale on the count back up. Doing this in public does make you look like serial killer, but it helps, and instills a sense of fear in strangers, so that's a bonus.

SERIOUSLY:
Anxiety is a problem but it can be treated over time. You might feel like crap, but you are not broken: you are you.

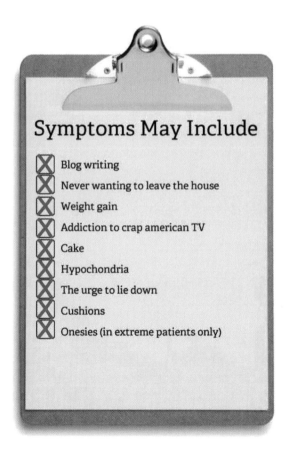

Symptoms May Include

- [x] Blog writing
- [x] Never wanting to leave the house
- [x] Weight gain
- [x] Addiction to crap american TV
- [x] Cake
- [x] Hypochondria
- [x] The urge to lie down
- [x] Cushions
- [x] Onesies (in extreme patients only)

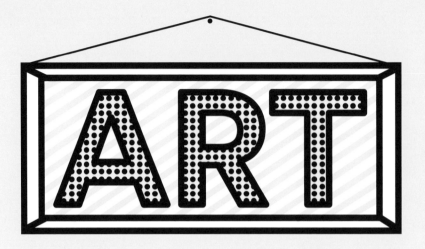

Stuff that looks like things. Or doesn't look like anything. Glad we cleared that up.

Art is one of those intangible things, which often means you can't decide whether something is a flowerpot in your nan's kitchen or an existential installation interpreting the scourge of Capitalism. SEE WHAT I MEAN?

If I were to staple a pheasant to my scrotum and stand in St Paul's Cathedral screaming 'Ave Maria', some might see this as artistic expression, others may suspect I am having a psychotic breakdown after a *Game of Thrones* spoiler.

'Why did he staple the pheasant to his balls?' one says.
'Why is he singing "Ava Maria"?' questions another
'This must be a statement about the poverty in western Italy,' a man says self-confidently, looking around to make sure someone heard his observation.

The art world is full of people who have shaved heads and poor housekeeping skills and basically turn colouring-in into multi-million pound profit. If someone had told me I could retire at 30 because of shading in bright yellow dots or having dirty sheets, I would be even more delusional than I am now. I'm not knocking art, it's just that I feel

for the next Rembrandt, who might be currently working in Tesco by day and producing masterpieces by night, and will never sell a single one.

I don't think anyone really understands art. I think most people are bluffing. It's something to do on a date to make you look like you have some cultural leanings and not like someone who mostly watches *Dog: The Bounty Hunter* re-runs in their spare time.

The Guide To Knowing Art

Portaits -	*Selfies that take ages to develop*
Renaissance art -	*Pictures of really boring people*
Contemporary art -	*A mess that takes six hours to explain*
Modern art -	*Like a toddler has gone mad on MS Paint*
Surrealism -	*Doing art while pretending to be on drugs*
Cubism -	*Everything looks like minecraft*
Impressionism -	*Stuff that actually kind of looks like stuff*
Pop art -	*Art for people who use Tumblr*
Installation art -	*Filling rooms with crap*

BELIEFS

Confidence in the existence of something, without any proof. Like love at first sight or vampires.

Beliefs are like sexual thoughts about horses. We all have them, but when you start telling other people about them they don't want to hang out with you anymore.

I tried to be an atheist for a bit. However, my general apathy for the works of Richard Dawkins, coupled with the fact that every atheist has spoken more about religion than any other religious person I have ever met, turned me off the idea. I am generally a believer in the idea that you can believe any fucking thing you want. You believe we came from two people who got kicked out of an orchard for scrumping? Fine. You believe we came from the armpit of a giant space ape whose gastric wind creates universes? Cool. Just be nice to other people about it.

'Don't be a twat' seems to be a piece of advice many people choose to ignore. If beliefs, religions or ideals are supposed to be those of love, law, morality and fairness, then don't be a prick about it. We might all be wrong. We may pass away, and the first thing we might see is two massive words in the sky saying 'Level Two'.

Most people find comfort in the fact that after this life there is something awaiting us, and I would like this to be true. I don't believe in heaven or hell, but I like to think that when our bodies decide to betray us and give up, that our thoughts go somewhere we deserve. Bad people have to sit through endless screenings of Adam Sandler movies, and good people get to sit in a massive cocktail lounge,

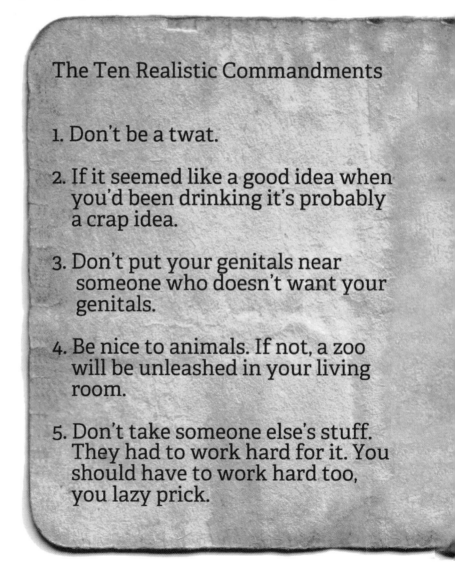

The Ten Realistic Commandments

1. Don't be a twat.

2. If it seemed like a good idea when you'd been drinking it's probably a crap idea.

3. Don't put your genitals near someone who doesn't want your genitals.

4. Be nice to animals. If not, a zoo will be unleashed in your living room.

5. Don't take someone else's stuff. They had to work hard for it. You should have to work hard too, you lazy prick.

your favourite band playing, waiting for your family to turn up and catch up on the last how many years.

Believe in what you want, but be nice to other people about it. If what someone else believes in isn't hurting you, isn't causing you or your family physical pain, then just follow Commandment 1.

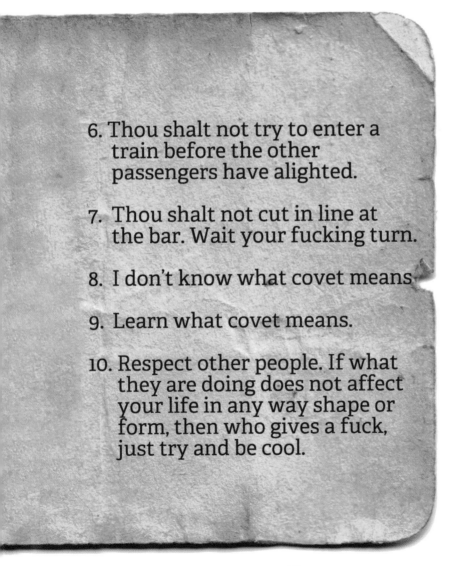

6. Thou shalt not try to enter a train before the other passengers have alighted.

7. Thou shalt not cut in line at the bar. Wait your fucking turn.

8. I don't know what covet means

9. Learn what covet means.

10. Respect other people. If what they are doing does not affect your life in any way shape or form, then who gives a fuck, just try and be cool.

BILLS

*Pieces of paper that let you
know how poor you are.*

After school, your life becomes a series of numbers. Numbers that are usually in the negative and in big red letters on a piece of paper delivered to your door by a man in a suit. We are so lucky that during our educative years we learn how to become financially responsible. That we have lessons on pensions and libraries filled with books on how to pay taxes instead of teaching us things that we will never use in the real world, like religious education or teamwork.

Personal Bank Statement

Aaron Gillies
Flat 2, ███████████

███████

Acct no: ███████
Sort Code: ███████

Netflix	£7.99
Water	£15.17
Gas	£50.13
Electricity	£48.78
Phone	£37.99
Gay Porn	£10.99
The men crying at uninterested women Hotline	£1969.32
TV License	£10.31
Rent	£9999999.99
Subscription to What Horse magazine	£10.99

The grown-up, adult and most sensible way to deal with bills is to have a special place in your house where you put the post at the end of the day. You then leave it there for weeks, months, feeling it staring at you.

The only time to open your bills is when a letter comes through with a thick red Times New Roman font on the front of it.

But surely the most unfathomable, EXTORTIONATE and unreasonable bill we will ever receive is our monthly modern mobile phone bill.

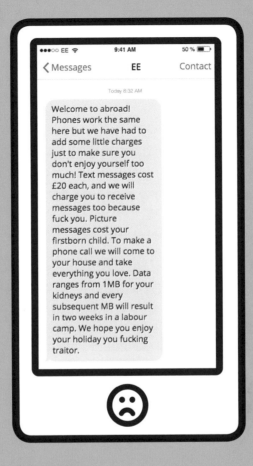

A BRIEF HISTORY OF MONEY:

The first signs of trading shit for other shit started over 100,000 years ago when societies would trade barley or wheat or velociraptors or something (I am not a historian) for other goods. The first use of coins was by the Lydians, who were all called Lydia, the first banks were in 2,000BC, which operated solely in beans or buttons, and the first case of paper money was noted by Marco Polo, who invented being blind in swimming pools. People have been billing people for as long as they could. It's now entrenched into our society that if you want something you have to pay for it, which is fundamentally against my life plan.

You will never be able to escape the people who want to charge you for things.

BODY IMAGE

What everyone tells you you should look like,
when you are OK just as you are. Except you.

The perfect human doesn't exist. Mostly because humans don't have wings and can't shoot chocolate out of their hands.

People look different and it is AWESOME. You don't need to 'CONFORM' to a 'SOCIAL NORM' and at 'SOME' point during this 'SENTENCE' you will figure out I 'DON'T' know how to use quotation marks properly. It is difficult to love yourself, not in the 15-year-old with-the-house-to-himself sort of way, but in a way in which YOU can find peace within your own skin.

As long as you are healthy, and what you are doing to your body isn't going to kill you, then who gives a flying fuck? Every body is beautiful, every body has its slight imperfections and its wobbly bits. Obsessing about this will not only take up a lot of your time, but it can make you really fucking boring on social media. Last month, a family from Exeter sent out a search party as their son hadn't checked in on Facebook to the gym he always goes to. Scientists have revealed that if you don't post your running stats on Twitter every day then you can slowly DIE.

Beauty is in the eye of the beholder, which is a great mantra for beekeepers but lets the rest of us down. Our differences in appearance keep us sane; if everyone was a clone of the perfected Hollywood Barbie and Ken model then we would go mad. Our conversations would be filled with gluten-free sheds and quinoa-scented candles.

And when the average women's magazine looks like this, how are you supposed to feel normal?

~B

BLOODY AWFUL

MEN?
How to set fire
to men in 20
different ways

SEX
Have you had
it 20 times today?

Kids or Dogs?
Which will get
you more
facebook likes?

You look so old

How you
are doing
everything
wrong

WOMEN
RICHER
THAN
YOU
WEARING
THINGS

WHY WOMEN
LAUGH AT SALADS
And how shampoo
makes you orgasm
for some reason

"I DIDN'T INSTAGRAM MY DINNER"
Real problems from real readers

BRITAIN

The Greatest Country on Earth that
is situated at 53.8260° N, 2.4220° W.

Everything the rest of the world thinks about us is true. We are obsessed with queueing and the weather, often combining the two, much to our dismay but gleeful in the knowledge that we will have a story about the weather to bore our co-workers with at a later date. We are a nation of beer drinkers, festival goers, tea slurpers and wasp haters. Our 70s DJs are not to be discussed and our politics are too fucked not to. We are a country of pride, who enjoy nothing more than mocking other British people.

A Google search entering the words [County is] and letting Google autocomplete finish the sentence gives us this:

Stereotypes are there for a reason and as Brits we lend ourselves to all of the tropes we have given ourselves. We apologise more than the Canadians and we are ruder than the French. We are greedier than the Americans and lazier than the Spanish.

However, being British is one of the finest things in the world. We get to drink our tea with our little finger out for no real reason. We have the NHS, Led Zeppelin, Hobnobs, roast dinners, ale, the BBC, fish and chips, Bendybus Cumbletrap and rain. It is fucking glorious! Of course we do also have loads of paedophiles and a government hellbent on killing the working class but you can't have everything.

Yet the British public will not be truly happy until the SAS find Diana and Maddie hidden somewhere in the BBC and Princess Kate shoots the perpetrators with a cannon that fires corgis and Jaffa Cakes.

WHAT ARE BRITISH VALUES?

Laughing at old people falling over
Not trusting your neighbours
Watching *Dr Who* even though it's
been crap for ages
Being scared to go outside
Man flu
Running from pigeons
Drinking tea even when it's really bloody hot
Not trusting the Welsh
Having a BBQ when it's raining
Apologising for something that isn't your fault
The Falklands

CAPITAL CITIES

The part of a country full of people who wish they live in other parts of the country.

All capital cities suffer from the same problem. They are ego farms, more expensive than the rest of the country and for no particular reason. The people are ruder, the dining is better, the subway is horrible and every street is as busy as a gym on 1st January. Yes, some capital cities differ; Paris is like one massive Café Rouge, where all the staff hate you. New York is like a city-wide game of *Supermarket Sweep* and no one is winning. Tokyo is a mescaline trip while you stare at a lava lamp. Edinburgh is what happens when you put a load of drunk people in a farmers market. Abu Dhabi is like every capital city but with its knob out, shouting, 'MINE IS BIGGER!'

In London you are never more than ten metres away from someone who claims to work in media. You can navigate the city simply by going from chicken shop to chicken shop. This metropolis is a bustling crowded concrete mess mass with upmarket cocktail bars and coffee shops that look like a student dorm room.

Like other capitals, London is the playground of the rich. Human broom explosion Boris Johnson has seen to that. The young who work and live in London are being pushed out to make way for people with supercars and 24-carat pocket squares to have a holiday home. Real Londoners no longer live in London. You can now calculate the cost of a London pint by opening your wallet and saying, 'Well, that's not going to be enough.'

10 Facts You Didn't Know About London

1. London is 67% escalators and 33% complaining about escalators
2. All the pigeons are called Lord Grantham
3. Big Ben is the name of the bloke who lives behind the clock
4. You can get into most of the art galleries for free if you run past security
5. Wherever you go, a Pret a Manger will be no further than three steps behind you
6. There are more beards than people
7. The Thames is the most boring river in Europe
8. 72% of Londoners still have the plague
9. No one is really sure why anyone goes to Leicester Square
10. Accordions are illegal in Soho for some reason

London

Capital of England

Where politicians sit and waste money. Full of people off their tits on coffee whilst being completely miserable. Home of the London tube network, an underground nightmare created by Satan.
Everything costs four times as much as outside of London for no fucking reason

Area: Bloody massive. Too big.

Founded: Fucking ages ago.

Weather: All the BBC talk about.

Local Time: Who cares.

Population: Tossers.

Points of interest   View 15+ more

| Shit ferris wheel | Tower thing | Hall of wax bastards | Old age home | Bastard emporium |

CATS

*Hairy things that people who have
stopped having sex collect.*

Cats are devious. Cats are evil. Cats figured out their game plan early
in their evolution. At some point roughly about 10,000 years ago, a
feline mastermind realised that if it was to train a human to look after it,
it would never have to worry about predators, hunting or breeding ever
again. It figured out it could get free food, potential mates brought to its
feet and attention lavished upon it. All it needed was a bunch of idiots.

And that's where the Egyptians came in. They were already fairly
up there on the shitbag scale [insert tasteless biblical joke], and then
they started worshipping cats. It's reasonable to sympathise with
the ego of a cat if you remember that their great great great great
grand-parents were thought of as gods.

As they sat being pampered by kings and brushed by princesses,
cats had no need to acclimatise to the modern world. They
effectively turned into ancient tamagotchis, with no real purpose
on this earth but to be fed and praised.

As the years went by nothing changed. Cats still rule the lives of
millions of enslaved humans across the globe. The internet is awash
with pictures revering the evil gitbags. And what do cats do with this
absolute power? They put their arseholes in your face. Because they
know they can get away with it. They would stab you if they could,
but the daft fucks never evolved thumbs due to laziness.

As dogs learned to serve humankind as a protector and an ally,

Stupid head ↘

Ears ↙

Evil eyes →

←Git

Tongue → like sandpaper for NO REASON

Tail to knock stuff over with

↑ Feet to knock stuff over with

cats watched from afar, filled with disdain yet occasionally eating their own hair and then being sick on it for some stupid reason.

Not all cats are bad, of course; cat owners, however, are. Cat owners are to Instagram what new parents are to Facebook. In some cases it may be easier for people to simply carry their pets around with them, launch them at people in the street and shout, 'ISN'T IT LOVELY?' as the cat frantically tries to escape and rips the surprised pedestrian's epidermis to shreds.

CH...RES

Things our parents do with ease yet we have an existential crisis thinking about.

At school they never teach you how to prepare for modern life. While you are studying how to ask to go to the library in several languages, education never prepares you for the real problems you will have to overcome. Cleaning an oven. Descaling a kettle. Finding out the toaster has a little drawer at the bottom for crumbs. I found out about that when I was 27. And I was much happier living in blissful ignorance.

We need proper education about how a household works. Millions of children are leaving home, staring at the hoover and wondering what the fuck goes where. Is there a bag? Do I need to change the bag? Why isn't it working? What do you mean, it plugs into the wall? HOW IS THERE NOT AN APP FOR THIS? Thousands of young adults around the country are heaped in corners, suffering from PTFSD (Post-traumatic Fitted Sheet Disorder), a horrific condition that occurs when one tries to foolishly iron a fitted sheet.

Washing isn't much easier. Avoid using a washing machine at all costs. Trousers only need washing if they have a stain on them. Pants and shirts need changing daily. Hoodies can survive for years. I don't know about bras, but I imagine they can survive for months.

So here to help is an easy guide to washing machine symbols for all those who, like me, are struggling with adulthood.

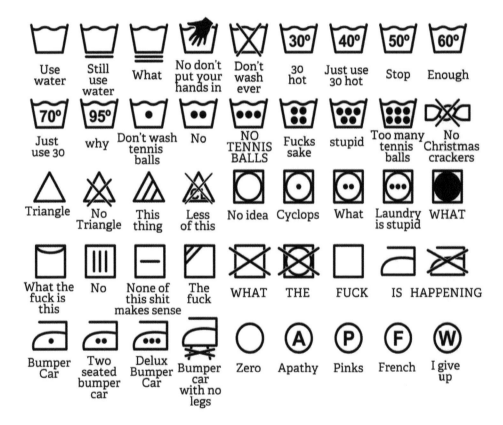

Use water	Still use water	What	No don't put your hands in	Don't wash ever	30 hot	Just use 30 hot	Stop	Enough
Just use 30	why	Don't wash tennis balls	No	NO TENNIS BALLS	Fucks sake	stupid	Too many tennis balls	No Christmas crackers
Triangle	No Triangle	This thing	Less of this	No idea	Cyclops	What	Laundry is stupid	WHAT
What the fuck is this	No	None of this shit makes sense	The fuck	WHAT	THE	FUCK	IS	HAPPENING
Bumper Car	Two seated bumper car	Delux Bumper Car	Bumper car with no legs	Zero	Apathy	Pinks	French	I give up

COFEEEEEE

Have you ever tried to do some work without coffee? It's like trying to read *War and Peace* while Andrew Neil sings the hits of Ed Sheeran at you. Basically, it's torturous. Coffee lets you procrastinate but REALLY FAST, AND WITH YOUR BRAIN IN CONSTANT CAPSLOCK. Some people don't drink coffee. These people are possibly Communist spies or have severe heart conditions. That is the only two explanations for this bizarre flaw in character.

THERE ARE MANY TYPES OF COFFEE:
INSTANT: Like cocaine mixed with flour.
POSH COFFEE: Like trying to have a good night on one ecstasy tablet while covered in frothy milk.
FILTER COFFEE: Like pouring Red Bull in your eyes.

The question is why would you ever take drugs when you can drink 17 coffees in a morning and be found screaming at the microwave because it's not printing anything.

It isn't just the painfully physical effects coffee creates within you that make it superior to tea, it's the class that goes with it. Drinking a latte in your driveway makes you feel like you're sitting on a street in Paris. Drinking a black filter coffee makes you feel like a lawyer in a 1960s drama. Drinking an espresso makes you feel like a giant. It's all about style, and getting off your tits on ground beans can make you feel like a god. You can post that you're drinking coffee al fresco in Soho, as this sounds classy, when what you're really doing is drinking a Subway flat white while sat on the street outside a Piccadilly strip club.

~C

EEEEEEEEEE

Cocaine for people who can't afford cocaine.

Remember, you can get the coffee shop experience at home by writing your name incorrectly in sharpie on your kettle before pouring a drink.

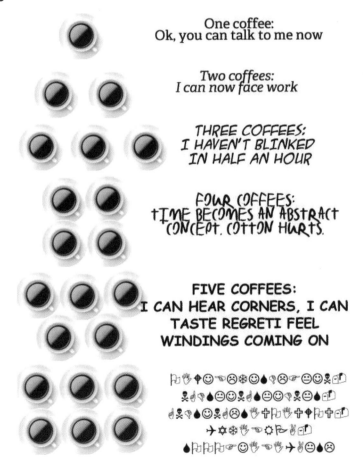

One coffee:
Ok, you can talk to me now

Two coffees:
I can now face work

THREE COFFEES:
I HAVEN'T BLINKED
IN HALF AN HOUR

FOUR COFFEES:
TIME BECOMES AN ABSTRACT
CONCEPT. COTTON HURTS.

FIVE COFFEES:
I CAN HEAR CORNERS, I CAN
TASTE REGRETI FEEL
WINDINGS COMING ON

THE DAILY MAIL

The media equivalent of…
Feel free to think of your own analogy.
It's just awful.

Someone with more time and patience than me could write an entire book on *The Daily Mail*. The only problem is that this book would make you so angry you'd sit down with a cup of tea to read it, then wake up four hours later with everything on fire and no memory of what happened.

 The Daily Mail is a newspaper that perceives itself as the last bastion of normality in an otherwise debauched world. Its values lay in an image of a fantasy Britain, where 'Land of Hope and Glory' plays in the background of every life. Where white people wave good morning at each other while they walk their perfect little family to the shops and back. Where the only foreigners can be found in takeaway restaurants, and sexual depravity is best left to Conservative MPs. It's a publication that remembers fondly a nation that never existed.

If *The Daily Mail* could be personified as a human being, it would be a 50-year-old man, slightly balding, slightly out of shape, with a fixation on young women in bikinis and a hatred of change. So Paul Dacre basically.

THE DAILY MAIL AGE CHART FOR WOMEN:
0-0.5 — Bouncing
0.5-14 — All grown up
14-22 — Tired
22-30 — Haggard
30-38 — Ill
38+ — Horrific, oh God, why, WHY?

Unfortunately *The Daily Mail* is the second most read paper in the UK (behind *The Sun*. Remember, don't look directly at the sun, it can damage your eyes) and often, a lot of people's only source for news. Like many media outlets in today's dystopian future, its bias and scaremongering are it's main selling points. Telling people about the horrors of the outside world: Immigrants buying English tea, 'lesbian mothers', 'a celebrity' that doesn't want their photo taken, 'a middle-aged woman' who doesn't want children, 'pretty' much the seventh circle of hell.

But hate sells. Every time a *Daily Mail* journalist is given currency to rant about whatever middle-class thing annoyed them this week, 'Oh, my, the horse is on fire' 'My imported cheese went through Slough', 'I can't find my John Major Butt Plug' or WHATEVER it may be, the clicks go through the roof. *The Sun* keep Katie Hopkins on retainer because the art of pissing people off sells, and while the left sit seething into their soya vanilla lattes, the right clasp their claws together in glee, dreaming of a day that will one day be like a 1970s soap opera. If anyone from *The Daily Mail* is reading this, I would like the adjective before my name to be 'Curvy', if you don't mind.

DEPRESSION

A chemical imbalance in your brain that makes everything feel like a Bon Iver song.

I was diagnosed with depression six years ago, and since coming to terms with the fact that this is part of who I am, I have attempted, in small ways, to stop feeling sorry for myself.

I follow a lot of depression sufferers on Twitter and find their bravery and 'normality' inspiring, yet stigma is everywhere. Many people have told me to just cheer up, or 'get over it' then change the subject. The word 'mental' is still bandied around as an off-hand insult and used in tabloid papers.

I'm not comfortable with people's conception of me being mad. I still feel like I am failing when I fill my mouth with tablets in the morning. I keep expecting myself to be a normal, functioning member of society, a human being who can go through a normal daily routine without incident... But this is not how I was made. Every decision I make is an internal argument about how I can fuck this up. Every breath is a question about how I can disappoint someone. Every action is a quandary, minutes spent terrified of other people's feelings.

But I've found out that it's important to remember that you are just you. Some people have a knee that pops every now and again; some people have that weird spot on their arm that's been there for years; some people have really, really ugly genitals. Depression is part of you, but you can sure as hell make sure it doesn't control your life. Take everything day by day. Write. Talk to people. Try to do one thing a day that makes it feel like you've accomplished something, even if it's just tidying the kitchen or going for a walk. It may sound silly, but what are tiny things to everyone else can help immensely to those suffering from depression.

If someone you love is going through this just try and be there for them. I would be nothing without my wife looking after me, just asking

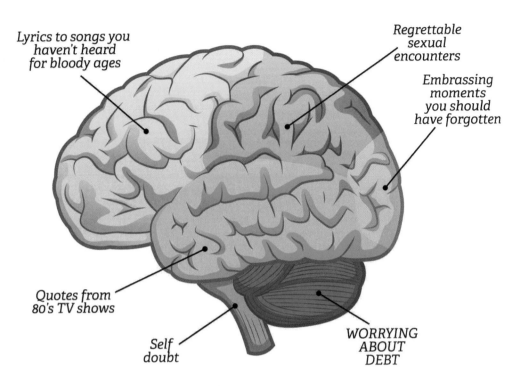

Lyrics to songs you haven't heard for bloody ages

Regrettable sexual encounters

Embrassing moments you should have forgotten

Quotes from 80's TV shows

Self doubt

WORRYING ABOUT DEBT

if I'm OK or if I need a drink. It doesn't need to be taxing to the other person; usually just knowing they are around can help.

Depression can be a selfish disease. You spend so much time focusing inwards that it is hard to be outgoing. You can spend a few days in bed, eating biscuits from the floor, wallowing, contemplating your own selfish existence, ignoring those around you to a point where you alienate everyone.

If you can't face the outside world, keep in contact with your friends. Don't push them away but don't keep people not worthy of your time near you. You have enough going on, you don't need additional bollocks in your life right now.

The hardest part of falling down is picking yourself back up.

That all got a bit serious for a moment, didn't it? Terribly sorry about that.

The Most Common Side Effects Of Antidepressants

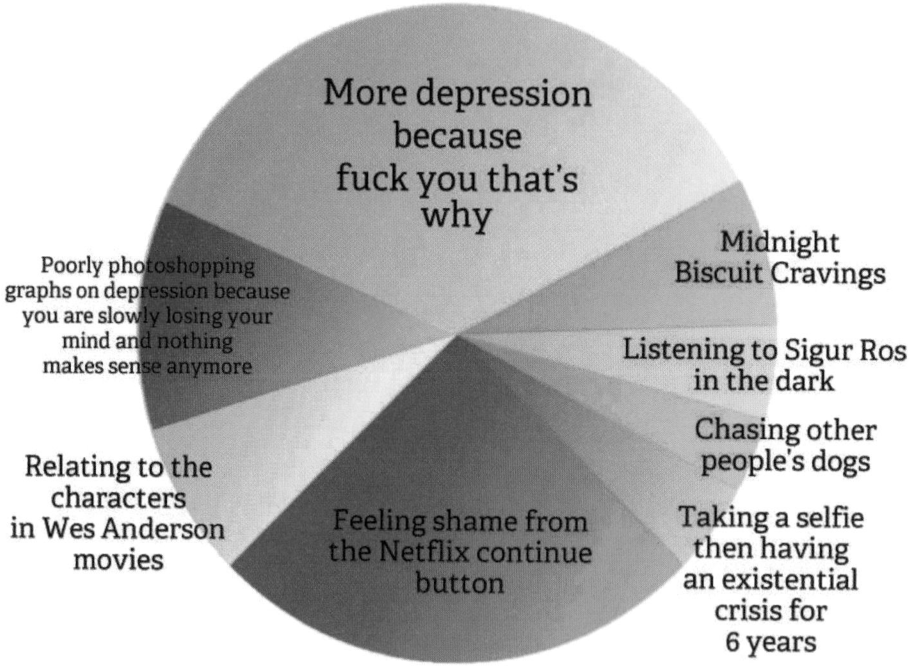

More depression because fuck you that's why

Midnight Biscuit Cravings

Poorly photoshopping graphs on depression because you are slowly losing your mind and nothing makes sense anymore

Listening to Sigur Ros in the dark

Chasing other people's dogs

Relating to the characters in Wes Anderson movies

Feeling shame from the Netflix continue button

Taking a selfie then having an existential crisis for 6 years

Literally the greatest thing ever.

You walk into a pub. There is a dog at the bar, there is a dog at a table with a bunch of people, there is a dog wandering up to strangers. This is the greatest bar ever! Now, change the word 'dog' with 'child' in that previous sentence, and you have yourself the worst bar ever.

When cats were deviously figuring out how to enslave the human race, dogs realised that humans were actually pretty OK, and decided we needed a hand with stuff. We needed a friend, not an overlord, and so our canine brethren came forth to save us from the tyranny of the feline menace.

We've all accidentally kidnapped a dog while walking along the street because it was looking at me and it loved me and it wanted to come home with me. It's just part of life.

There are no bad dogs, only bad owners. Because, yet again, humans inevitably ruin everything they touch. All dogs are good dogs. However, there are some serious questions that surround dogs that I require some answers to.

When I was about 21, I came home drunk and can't remember going to bed. I awoke in the dog's bed (Hendrix, German Shepherd, Maverick). In my drunken stupor Hendrix must have taken pity on me. He thought to himself, 'This twat won't be able to navigate the stairs, if I can get him to my bed, I'll have the sofa.' This is why dogs are brilliant: they look after you, know when you're sad, they know when you need them and they love you unconditionally.

Dogs are part of the family, they feel what you feel, they are pleased to see you and they are only happy when you are happy. If everyone in the world could love each other the way a dog loves you when you are bringing it food, the world would be a much better place.

DRUGS

Chemical substances that help you decide which of your friends you don't want to hang out with anymore.

How do you know if someone you know takes drugs? They haven't shut up about it since they got into your house three hours ago.

Recreational drugs can have many side effects. From finding the music of Mumford & Sons appealing, to ripping off your skin and attempting to star in your own George A. Romero film, they are all mostly horrific.

Doing drugs is kind of like being a Brony – yes, I am very aware you are proud of your identity, you have every right to abuse yourself in any way you choose as long as it doesn't affect other people, just make sure you aren't left alone with children or old people.

However, the Government are right about one thing: children should avoid drugs. They get everything for free as it is, including free room and board. God knows what they would do with free skank.

The benefits of legalising some drugs are fairly self-evident. A rise in corduroy trouser sales. Greater viewing figures for QVC and that religious channel where the man shouts about women. Park benches would almost be constantly occupied, and more students would start taking Chemistry.

If you are interested in taking drugs, please use the following guide:

WEED
Taken while listening to a Grateful Dead record while dressed like an explosion in a charity shop. Side effects can include the inexplicable need to never stop talking about weed. Wearing snapbacks in public.

COCAINE
Best taken while wearing a suit to a Rolling Stones' soundtrack in the 1980s. Side effects include shouting, screaming, running and having nostrils the size of an aircraft hanger.

ECSTASY
Best taken while on a night out, in an awful club, with awful music, with people you hate. Side effects include being a complete wanker, drinking lots of water and being a complete wanker.

MAGIC MUSHROOMS
Best taken at college, while surrounded by items your parents bought you, while revelling in your independence. Side effects can include sitting, wide eyes and the need to bring up the story about that one time you did magic mushrooms.

KETAMINE
Best taken under peer pressure from people who obviously hate you. Side effects include having your genitals removed to make room for a urine funslide.

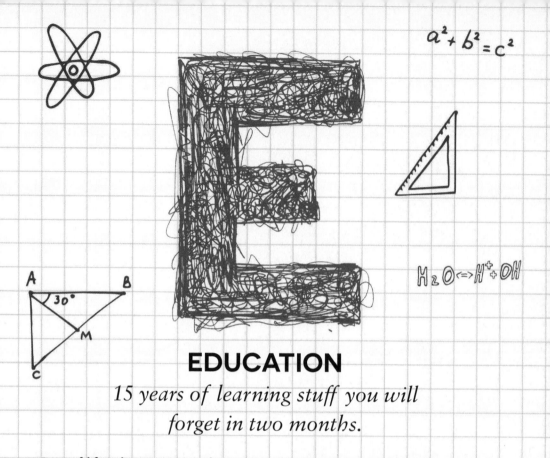

EDUCATION

15 years of learning stuff you will
forget in two months.

One of life's big ironies is that just at the time in your life when you are embarking on your first big milestone you can ALSO legally drink as much alcohol as you like for the first time. As everyone in your life tells you to make the choices that will define you for the rest of your life, shots of Jager are only 50p.

As kids, we are often asked what we want to be when we grow up. 'BATMAN' seems one of the more sensible options, which only goes to prove what a fucking stupid question it is to ask a kid. A much more useful question is: 'Do you want to own your own house and eat non-own-brand food when you grow up?' If I had known at eight years old exactly what working hard meant in terms of such luxuries, I would have spent less time drinking myself half to death around girls I found attractive and more time studying so that I could afford to drink myself half to death around women I found attractive. I could have saved myself a lot of time, and washing cycles.

Education has taught me at least one valuable skill. I know how to ask where the library is in French (which has proved a lifeline, as you can imagine) and how to put a condom on a banana. Education never taught me how to do my taxes without having a mild breakdown, or write a CV that didn't include the term 'sexual fiesta' and wasn't in Comic Sans, or how to interact with the general public at an acceptable level. If the Government would just leave the curriculum to the teachers who actually KNOW the kids they are teaching then an average school day might look something like this:

6.30 **1ST CLASS** Learning to wake up early, you lazy twats

7.30 Coffee, even if you are too young for coffee, just drink it

8.30 An hour on a busy train simulator

9.30 **2ND CLASS** Learning how to talk to people you hate

10.30 Fag break

10.45 **3RD CLASS** Advanced Netflix and ramen preparation

11.45 **4TH CLASS** Financial responsibility and coping with failure

12.45 Lunch

1.15 **5TH CLASS** Sexual Education and erasing your browser history

2.15 **6TH CLASS** Art and Music, and how you will forget about these when you get a job

3.15 **7TH CLASS** Maths and web coding, learning about internet validation

4.15 An hour on the busy train simulator

5.15 Pub logistics.

Elitism

The idea that some people are born better than others... well, you. I mean just... God, look at you.

Two men enter a restaurant, one is wearing £5,000 Gucci loafers, the other is wearing TK Maxx knock-off trainers. Who gets served first? That's right, the latter because this is a Wetherspoons and your stereotypes don't exist here.

It's perfectly healthy to hate the rich. In our Tory-driven time of austerity, when we have been instructed to eat Tesco value beans instead of Heinz, and to resort to witchcraft instead of using the NHS, it's infuriating to see men in suits, covered in wealth, laughing at the poor's expense.

When you are born into wealth, you go to better schools, you get better jobs, you eat swan for dinner and for your 15th birthday party

Why do we hate the rich?

Is it simply bred into the middle and lower classes to be wary of the elite? Are our aspirations of wealth simply a carrot dangled infront of the donkey that is society?

76%
of rich people have tried to pay homeless people to fight for their amusement

1/2
Of the Forbes 500 list are called Humphrey

£2.6bn
Was spent on caviar last year by Michael Gove alone

176
The real age of Donald Trump. Money makes you immortal

200
Chickens are sacrificed per year as part of the banks' archaic method of measuring interest

Mark
Zuckerberg doesn't know what a Greggs is

you get a prostitute and a cocaine party. For the other classes, a 15th birthday is usually a sad wank and a caterpillar cake. OK, in all fairness that sounds better than the upper-class alternative.

Hatred of the rich only falls upon those deemed unworthy of their own wealth. The Instagram kids shoving Bollinger down themselves, the reality TV stars throwing their genitalia at cameras, the MPs jeering at each other like monkeys on heat during Prime Minister's Questions. As the common person is told to work, and to work as hard as they can, the wealthy are shown to us as a goal, an unattainable goal, that we should be jealous of. Money is wasted on the rich.

ENVIRON MENTAL ISM

Caring more about plants and animals than humans because humans are just awful.

I signed a petition the other day to save the whales. Even though I had misread this as a petition to shave the Welsh, I still believe I have done my good deed for the year and can go back to poorly organising my recycling.

As we are basically monkeys in trousers sitting in concrete blocks on an asteroid hurtling around a gigantic space bomb, we take our planet for granted. Our planet is rejecting us. Australia is the perfect example of this: every plant and animal in Australia has evolved to try and kill humans. Even hedges have been known to eat people in their sleep. The polar ice caps are melting, which in turn will mean the end of the Coca-Cola bear and his family. The rainforests are dying, so in a decade students won't have anywhere to go to take pictures to put on Facebook. These are truly terrible times.

Our salvation lies in renewable energy. Windfarms are a good source of power and an excellent way of solving Britain's rabid giraffe crisis. Ever seen a giraffe near a windfarm? See. Solar power is a brilliant way of showing up just how selfish your neighbours are.

How Do Wind Turbines Work?

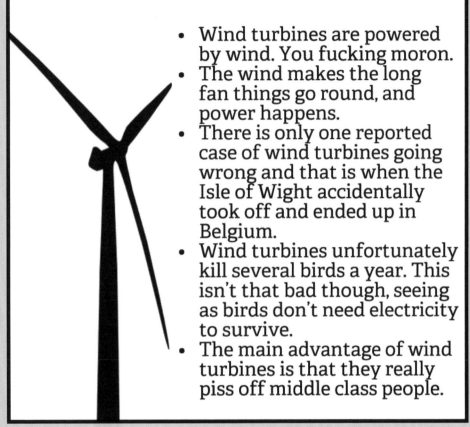

- Wind turbines are powered by wind. You fucking moron.
- The wind makes the long fan things go round, and power happens.
- There is only one reported case of wind turbines going wrong and that is when the Isle of Wight accidentally took off and ended up in Belgium.
- Wind turbines unfortunately kill several birds a year. This isn't that bad though, seeing as birds don't need electricity to survive.
- The main advantage of wind turbines is that they really piss off middle class people.

Gerbils in wheels are a fantastic way of showing those damn gerbils their place. Sea power is a sure-fire way to stop sharknados.

If more young people signed petitions online, our awareness of self-congratulatory Facebook posts would increase 200%, and this needs to be done.

We do need to give more of a shit. Nature doesn't deserve the rough hand we have dealt it. As per usual, humans turn up and ruin everything. Imagine the lifespan of the earth was condensed to a 24-hour day. Humans have turned up to the dinner party at one minute to midnight and accidentally set the house on fire.

EXPERIENCES

Something that should be done once,
and only once.

'I'll try anything once!' screamed the uninteresting person from the back of the crowd. Most of us will try anything once, because if we try it and don't like it, usually we don't feel the need to do it again. Like sticking your testicles in Marmite, it was probably a good idea at the time, but you wouldn't need to do it again. Alas, life is short, as many teen indie films tell us, and we have to live every day to the full for some fucking stupid reason.

Some people go bungee jumping, some people try to have sex with animals, and others go to Wales. Our sense of adventure is hard to dismiss. We all want to travel the world, wrestle a bear or drink a cocktail off an emperor's buttocks, but most of us are financially challenged, unambitious, and when the idea of two weeks off comes around, sitting in pyjamas while watching cartoons seems like a much more reasonable adult activity.

Would you rather have a large Facebook photo album of you doing selfies while lost in the Australian outback, or would you prefer to have enjoyed the moment, not worried about how it will look to your friends, who don't really care anyway? Experiences are individualistic: you experienced them, no one else, they are little moments in time that you can proudly call your own. That time you got drunk in a Thai hostel and accidentally spooned Big Jim the boatmaster? For you, that story is something special, for everyone else, it's that annoying story you tell every time the conversation comes around to travelling.

We overshare, we tag ourselves in proud situations online so that our friends can seethe with jealousy.

The best way to ensure that you experience life to the full is to make a bucket list. Something like mine per se?

Things I want to do before I die

Punch a shark

Punch Piers Morgan

Punch Piers Morgan with a shark

Eat an entire Victoria sponge in one go

Watch a Kevin James film without vomiting blood

Go to space

Pay my parents back the money they've given me

Buy a giraffe

Enter giraffe in the Grand National

Check my bank balance without crying

Create a robot

Send robot back in time to kill Hitler

Watch Scotland win the 6 Nations

Build something from IKEA without a breakdown

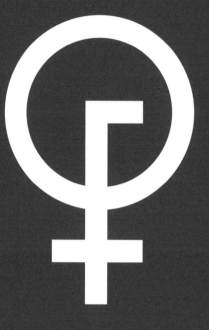

FEMINISM

Oh... I am going to fuck this up so badly!

Why am I a feminist? Because everybody was a shit to Ripley in the *Alien* films and she was the only one who had a fucking clue. All the dinosaurs in *Jurassic Park* were female, and men tried to contain them so they fucked shit up. Black Widow is the only Avenger with a clue. Princess Leia choked a gigantic snail thing to death while wearing a bikini, at the same point where all the men were busy almost getting eaten by a giant sand vagina. SEE.

Just under 100 years ago women weren't allowed to vote, now they can become Ghostbusters. We have really advanced as a society. 'What next?' the scared men screamed, 'WOMEN LAWYERS. WOMEN CATS. WOMEN LEARNING TO READ. WHERE WILL IT END?' It won't end. Soon women will be everywhere; in our supermarkets, our workplaces. Scientists say that in 20 years they might even be in our homes.

Imagine if you will a universe where men get treated like women.

The *Daily Mail* is filled with images of side scrote and Prince George being called a slut. Young men have to walk home with their keys between their fingers in case a group of drunken women approach them. Every time they seem a bit grumpy it's probably just because they are manstrating. A woman slaps your dick on the bus and winks at you and no one helps.

As a man (he shouted in the section about feminism without the slightest bit of irony) I would not call myself a Male Feminist. Simply a man who supports feminism. I don't think men should correct women on their feminism; we shouldn't critique the movement or mock. We need to be educated, because men are stupid hairy creatures. Remember, if you don't support feminism you are wrong, and being wrong is for women.

FIFTY SHADES

Porn for people who don't understand sex.

WARNING: This film contains ADULT THEMES such as bills, work, trying to be healthy, being miserable and debt.

The thing that really bothers me is that it's fine for you to read *Fifty Shades of Grey* while on the bus in the morning but I read a copy of *Tentacle hentai #37* and I am called a pervert. *Fifty Shades of Grey* is porn for people who don't understand what sex is. Imagine you haven't had sex for quite some time (some of you don't have to imagine do you? HAHAHAHAHAAH! Oh, I made myself sad) and they publish a book that says, 'You know what, this is what sex is nowadays' And it makes you a bit hot under the collar because back in your day it was missionary for 12 minutes then a cigarette and *Coronation Street*. Kids today are using whips and water boarding and anal grenades and you haven't seen anyone else's genitals in six years. It's all terribly exciting, isn't it?

THIS IS WHAT HAPPENS WHEN MIDDLE-CLASS PEOPLE TRY TO TAKE SEXUAL INSPIRATION FROM FAUX PORN LIKE FIFTY SHADES ➡

There are other socially acceptable ways to watch pornography. You can just be sitting in the front room with your parents, watching a light-hearted action comedy, THEN SUDDENLY a sex scene happens. You don't know where to look. Your parents don't know where to look. You all just stare at the family dog for no reason while two people bang in the background. And you never speak of this again. Men can just buy a lads mag to be able to look at porn which is well within the realms of normality for some reason. Women can buy... home and garden magazines. What do women like? Instagram and knives. Think that's it.

'Keith, I've just finished a chapter in *Fifty Shades of Grey* I think we should try.'

Keith turns from the repeat of *Top Gear*, wipes away the Wotsits from his mouth and says, 'Sounds great, let me do some stretches.'

'I'll meet you in the bedroom,' Sandra whispers.

Keith goes into the bedroom and sees Sandra on the bed.

'I want you to tie me up.'

'With what?' Keith enquires.

'Some rope,' Sandra replies seductively.

'We don't have any rope, no one just keeps rope around the house.'

'Then one of your ties.'

Keith goes to the wardrobe and tries to find his ties. He hasn't worn them in years after the fire.

'Which tie?'

'The black one,' Sandra whispers

'The one I wore to your grandma's funeral?'

'OK, not that one, the blue one,'

'I was going to save that for Brian and Tess's wedding next weekend.'

'The other one then,' Sandra replied.

'The only other one is from Tony and it was a present, I don't really want to crease it,' he moaned seductively.

They didn't bother having sex because they were both knackered from talking about ties. Keith went back to his Wotsits.

FITNESS

*The act of self-enforced torture to obtain
a body people want to do a sex on.*

THE GYM

You pay £50 to stand in clothes you have recently purchased to
make it seem like you know what you are doing. A man who is
physically superior to you in every way walks you around some
machines that look like transformers that got stuck while having a
stroke. This man then shouts at you as you contort yourself into
these machines and make a fool of yourself.

SWIMMING

In the act of swimming you have to expose body parts that you
aren't even comfortable with your partner seeing while you are
trying to dry yourself after a shower in the morning. You plunge into
a hole in the ground filled with industrial chemicals and the fluids of
other people's children and attempt to direct your body at the other
end of the pool while looking like an overweight goose traversing a
river of treacle.

RUNNING

I had heard that running is effective and free therapy for those with
MH disorders. I tried it. I tried to enjoy it, I really did. I bought the
shoes. I launched myself down my road. My headphones kept falling
off. My keys flung around in my front pocket enough to make it look
like my penis was trying to escape. I huffed. I puffed. And I blew
things out of my face I didn't know existed. I got home as a red
sweaty mess and had never been more attractive.

WEIGHTS

If God had wanted humans to lift heavy things over and over again for no reason then She would have given us robot arms. But She didn't. The only people who find weights interesting are those who use the word 'bro' as a pronoun. You sit on a sweaty bench, covered in other people's arse juices, lifting a thing until your arms feel like wet spaghetti. The goal? BIG ARMS. I don't want to look like Stretch Armstrong on steroids, I am quite happy looking like a pillow filled with mince with toothpicks sticking out of it.

FROM MY ONE EXPERIENCE INSIDE A GYM, HERE IS A QUICK GUIDE TO GYM EQUIPMENT:

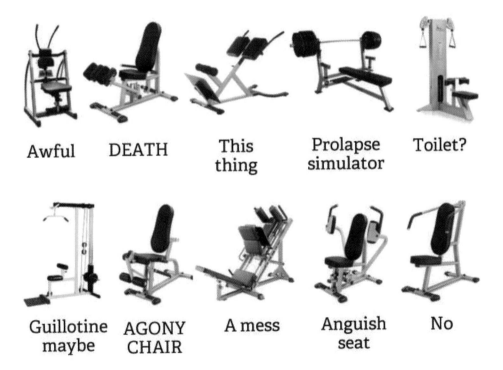

Awful   DEATH   This thing   Prolapse simulator   Toilet?

Guillotine maybe   AGONY CHAIR   A mess   Anguish seat   No

If you'll excuse me I am going to have a cigarette and an entire cake because I am an adult and can make my own poor life choices. (The cake thing was on my bucket list, it is entirely justified.)

FRANCE

Prendre à droite à la bibliothèque pour trouver la piscine.

As the UK falls out with Scotland, and Russia and the EU – pretty much everyone really – we could almost forget our sworn enemy, the French.

They eat good food. Their alcohol doesn't make you want to climb into a bin and die. It's a disgusting way of life and one we are jealous of. The Brits hate the French and that's that. Like the neighbour your parents irrationally dislike, and make fun of while sat in the safe comfort of their own home.

In France, most people are 78% croissant, 22% cheese & onion. Their children scream poetry at each other in the street, their elders throw garlic at tourists and reminisce about publicly murdering royalty.

But the really awful, UNFORGIVEABLE thing about the French is their BLOODY MUSIC, which can be divided into two categories:

1. Sting. If Sting were a drug, he would be prescribed as a method of your body rejecting your ears.
2. Someone shouting in French over heavy kick drums. These songs go on for decades and are like listening to a robot orgasm in a skip. Possibly the reason the French go on strike so often.

~F

GADGETS

*Tiny things we carry in our hands
that help us to ignore people.*

Science will have only gone too far when there is an app that shoots biscuits at you from the other side of the room, and you can purchase more biscuits from the online store. And 3D print biscuits maybe. Or a Grindr-style app but for people near you who have biscuits. But until this happens I think we are at a good stage of technological innovation. Excuse me, I am really craving biscuits...

...

...

OK.

You can take the chip out of your Oyster card, put it under the skin on your palm and jedi your way through the London Underground. You can attach a fleshlight to an iPad and learn to become infinitely lonely. There are apps that can control your kettle and your fridge, so you need never prise yourself out of your armchair but can simply concentrate on your goal of achieving optimum mass.

Technology does, however, have its drawbacks. The other day my book, my tape player, my watch and my cigarette all ran out of battery and I was left standing in a coffee shop in a state of complete and utter bereavement. I began screaming jokes in 140 characters or less at strangers, expecting them to put a gold star on me or to shout the joke back at their friends, but all that happened was I got banned from all the Pret A Mangers in Zone 1.

Are we too obsessed with technology? Do we rely on computers too much? Yes, obviously, because it's fucking brilliant! Those who despise our new-fangled gadgets are not allowed to have sex with robots when that becomes a thing. Because that is definitely going to become a thing.

The older generations will say that our generation is too obsessed with gadgets, apps, iThis and iThat. However, their generation was obsessed with wars, financial crises and Margaret Thatcher so I think we get the better deal there.

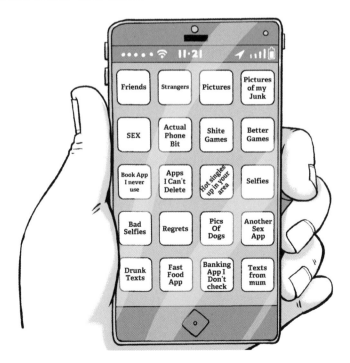

GAMBLING

♦ ♥ ♠ ♣

Losing your money on purpose.

You can bet on anything. You can bet on which government will get into power, which walking sob story will win the next big reality TV show, a fox hunt, genocide, anything. In my life I have won two things, the first being 500 dollars on a gambling machine in New Zealand, and the second being a 'Human Disaster' award at the Edinburgh Fringe. I play the Lottery, but it would appear all of my friends and family were born on the wrong days of the month. I went to bingo once and realised my failure at GCSE Maths may be more of a brain injury than a lack of intelligence. The one year I bet on the Grand National all of the horses I bet on were shot. I have since decided gambling isn't for me.

Most of us are already content gambling in more middle-class ways, like not reading our car insurance documentation all the way through, or eating a burger from a petrol station.

If I had more money I would probably make men in suits run down Bishopsgate for my amusement, but until then I will continue to gamble by not properly paying attention when I cook chicken.

The most depressing places in the UK are inside betting shops. The floor sticky with sweat, the tiny pens covered in chip grease, the men with 20 eyebrows eyeing you up as you tiptoe your way over the crisp packets and false teeth.

Instead of betting on sporting events, why not bet on things happening in your own life? Put odds on when Steph from sixth form is going to have her 16th ugly child. Bet on which of your friends will become an alcoholic first. Keep it interesting, and if the worst comes to worst and you need to gamble, simply tape £50 notes to Golden Retrievers and throw a ball into the distance. This is real sport.

Royal Flush
Best one

| A ♥ | K ♥ | Q ♥ | J ♥ | 10 ♥ |

FLUSH
Good yeah ok not bad, nice, yeah, sweet

| 8 ♣ | 7 ♣ | 6 ♣ | 5 ♣ | 4 ♣ |

THIS ONE
Like winning in Go Fish

| 5 ♦ | 5 ♠ | 5 ♥ | 5 ♣ | 3 ♥ |

Three of a card and two of a card
Makes five of a card

| K ♥ | K ♦ | K ♠ | 5 ♥ | 5 ♣ |

Running flushing run
When you get all the soots to match up

| K ♣ | J ♠ | 9 ♣ | 7 ♠ | 3 ♣ |

Run
If you get this hand, run from the table

| Q ♠ | J ♦ | 10 ♣ | 9 ♠ | 8 ♥ |

Threesome
Like all threesomes in real life, quite disappointing

| Q ♣ | Q ♦ | Q ♦ | 5 ♠ | 9 ♣ |

Two pairs
The swingers hand. Most people who get this hand have been unhappy in their marriage for quite some time

| K ♥ | K ♠ | J ♣ | J ♦ | 9 ♦ |

One pair
Worst. Awful. You are shit at this game

| A ♣ | A ♦ | 9 ♥ | 6 ♠ | 4 ♦ |

GENTRIFICATION

Or when rich people invade.

This morning I woke up to find my kitchen had been gentrified. Now I can no longer afford to go in there and it's full of wankers wearing flannel shirts and spending their parents' money. Where once there was a humble toaster now sits a 17-slice bespoke bagel warmer. My kettle has been replaced with a coffee machine that looks like a transformer's kidney stone.

As rich people priced themselves out of their own areas, they stalked the lesser-known areas of our cities, the areas where communities have come together, where nothing really special happens, where everyone knows Jim the guy at the greasy spoon and stabbings aren't as frequent as they used to be. The rich see these places and whip out their wallets, screaming 'NOPE' at the locals and in two weeks the high street is selling Louis Vuitton babygros, gluten-free hammocks and yacht insurance.

The rich areas are now empty, mansions lay reserved as holiday homes for billionaires from overseas who don't like our city enough to live here but still need somewhere to do cocaine off a Tory peer's leg once a year. The locals get pushed out to make way for a better way of life for the few. In certain areas of London if you are caught drinking a pint out of a pint glass you'll be bombarded with jam jars until you've learnt your lesson.

Most of us are happy with a baker's that doesn't cook rats into the bread, a pub where you can leave with all your teeth and a cinema with a screen bigger than Chaining Tattoo's weird square head. As the ladies who lunch march the streets at 11am, looking for somewhere that serves babyccinnos so Heidi-Sue-Chrysanthemum-BJ the 4th (or whatever rich people call their spawn) can shut the fuck up for two minutes, we lose a little bit of the city's soul.

~G

ONLY YOU
CAN PREVENT
GENTRIFICATION

KEEP AN EYE OUT FOR:
- SKINNY JEANS
- INDEPENDENT DELIS
- BOOKSHOPS
- GLUTEN-FREE PUBS
- BASTARDS

KEEP YOUR NEIGHBOURHOOD
THAT LITTLE BIT SHIT.
SAY NO TO YUMMY MUMMIES.
SAY NO TO COCKTAILS IN
MASON JARS.
SAY NO TO FOXTONS.

BE VIGILANT

G I R L S

I like my coffee like I like my women, strong enough to kill me but with a hint of mercy.

Girls, in fact all females of the species, are AWESOME and can do EVERYTHING. MEN just cry at sports and shout out of vans.

Men are terrified of women from a young age. So to make up for this they act like complete cocks to make every woman ever know that THEY ARE A MAN and REALLY MANLY and do MANLY THINGS. Men are awful! Men are basically a social experiment that went terribly wrong and no one has been able to get it back under control. If men had to deal with periods every month, they would get time off work, money, cuddles and you can be damn sure tampons wouldn't be taxed. But we don't, so it's fine. I'm sure it's not that bad. Ever been kicked in the balls? It hurts for LITERALLY seconds. You will never know this pain.

If I have learnt anything from adverts and unnecessarily gendered products, it's that women enjoy many things. Smiling at yoghurt. Wearing summer dresses in the rain and spinning around. Keeping calm and carrying something. They also enjoy shaving legs that have already been shaved, talking about wine on Facebook but then never actually drinking wine when you meet up with them, and posting pictures of books on Instagram. That is all you will ever need to know about women. With this information you will be married within minutes.

Jokes about women are great too, though. Yeah? Like, 'Why was the blonde staring at the orange juice? Because she was a young professional woman who wanted to know the nutritional information of what she was choosing to ingest', for example.

However, there will always be one mystery surrounding women:

What The Fuck Are These Things?

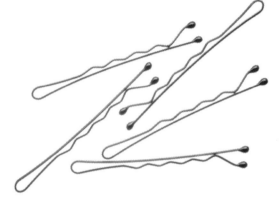

Location:
Fucking everywhere
Can be found:
Where wife has been
Use:
Unknown
Possible Uses:
Tiny chopsticks?
Paper clip?
Shit violin
Lockpick
Robot pube.

What we know:
They breed exponentially.
Never to be found in the same place twice.
Cannot be killed.
If you throw one away, three take its place.

Plan of action:
Kill the mothership. All others may die. If this fails, set house on fire. Plan C, call the science people.

HOME

Hutches for people.

When you grow tired of living in the same house that your parents once copulated in, you try and leave home – you fly the nest and wallow in your independence. Then you realise that, although you can stay up all hours and masturbate yourself into a frenzy, living by yourself is in fact mainly debt, solitude and completely unwelcome responsibility. You just end up wanting to move home.

Our homes reflect ourselves. Some nests are pristine and clean with wipe-clean sofas, and others are clusterfucks of dumpsters with more filth than a dildo-testing laboratory. This is when you look for a plate in the washing up and something winks at you from the bowl.

After a while you grow up a bit and realise that your home is your space and something to be proud of and show other people occasionally.

The different types of property: A Foxtons Guide

Detached
A property that doesn't touch another property. For wealthy customers only.

Semi-Detached
A property with one neighbour. This neighbour should usually be loud and have sex at stupid bloody times of the day.

Flat
Like a house but with two rooms and a shower that leaks all the time and basically a cupboard.

Terraced
When loads of houses are chucked together and you are squidged in the middle.

Bungalow
Like a cottage but for OAPs

Tent
Mobile and cheap property

Hut
Also known as a shed. Mostly used for Londoners and students. Rents start at £1000pw

Castle
Houses with 2 or more bedrooms. Possibly running water.

Bin
The most affordable properties for rent, reserved for students and people that actually need decent sized houses but fuck those guys.

The physical feeling of regret.

The proverb 'You Are What You Eat' is incorrect. It should be 'You Are What You Drink'. The greatest anecdotes do not start with 'This one time when I ate one too many sandwiches', they start with 'There was this one time when I was banjaxed off my hoofs'.

The trouble with being banjaxed off your hoofs is that when you wake up the next day you feel like a hairy, neglected wardrobe in a skip. This is known as a hangover.

The drinking part is fun; it takes the edge off life's crap. If you're cripplingly shy, it makes you able to talk to people, interesting people, people you'd usually only see from behind a bush outside their house. If you're worried about something, it makes the worry fade to a blur. If you're at a wedding, it makes that boring accountant sat next to you almost interesting. In other words, booze is awesome. It makes everyone a scholar and a jester at the same time.

AND THEN YOU WAKE UP.

And you're pretty much back to square one.

If you're new to drinking, however, and want to adopt the right beverage for your personality, here's a list of drinks and drinkers. See anyone you know?

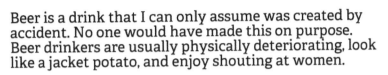

Beer is a drink that I can only assume was created by accident. No one would have made this on purpose. Beer drinkers are usually physically deteriorating, look like a jacket potato, and enjoy shouting at women.

Vodka drinkers are either 20 years old, poor and under the delusion that they can handle alcohol, or 45 years old and can drink like a Russian sailor at Oktoberfest.

Gin drinkers usually wear flowery skirts, stupid bloody hats and imagine themselves as the centre of a Nabokov novel.

Whisky drinkers fall into two categories, 25-year-old men with beards who hate whisky, or elderly men with large foreheads who guzzle it down like dehydrated giraffes at a water hole.

Wine drinkers are the most pretentious. Sniffing their drinks like a dog at a drug bust, lying to themselves and everyone else around them about the fact that they just want to chuck it down their face.

Those who choose to afflict their bodies with Jagerbombs are effectively shouting 'YOU WILL HAVE FUN YOU TWAT' at you via the medium of liquid.

Rum drinkers are in most cases poor, have developed gout at some time in their life and like to say things like "Oh they don't have blah, blah. blah. bottle x blah, blah, blah" hoping that anyone in the vicinity gives a flying shit.

Cocktails are alcoholic drinks for people who hate alcohol. People who cannot stand the taste of a spirit but have the need to scream at their friends in the street at 1am.

HOMEOPATHY

*Like medicine
but for Hogwarts' students.*

The UK's Minister of Health believes in homeopathy, but the House of Commons Science Committee has said that there is no evidence that homeopathy works, and the NHS website states implicitly the whole thing is bollocks. It's basically witchcraft for middle-class people.

But if you're thinking of trying alternative medicine, here's some actual bollocks:

LEECHES Not a cure for anything, only good for throwing at your neighbour's cat when it pisses in your back garden.

ACUPUNCTURE Basically... needles. You can recreate acupuncture at home by sticking paperclips into your forehead and then flushing a £50 note down the toilet.

MEDITATION Daydreaming with your legs crossed. You can recreate this at home by daydreaming with your legs crossed.

While researching homeopathy, I found some hilarious websites offering alternative treatments for the effects of stuff like anthrax, which was basically 'wait for it to go away or kill you'. And another site actually said that a good way of getting rid of STDs was through PRAYER.

A Homeopathy Guide

If you are considering using Homeopathy in any way, shape or form please contact your GP. The use of Homeopathy can be dangerous and addictive.

Wanting to try and use homeopathic methods can be a sign of fatigue, hallucinations or severe breakdown.

If you or any member of your family have been affected by Homeopathy, please contact your nearest surgery or hospital.

EVERY YEAR DOZENS OF PEOPLE TRY HERBAL REMEDIES. EVERY YEAR DOZENS OF PEOPLE DIE. THESE TWO FACTS MAY NOT BE RELATED, OR COULD THEY?

HUMANS

*Like monkeys but with credit cards
and caffeine addictions.*

I am not a scientist, but the following facts about human evolution are 100% true:

First came single-celled organisms, which were about as useful as eyelashes on a Ford Fiesta. Then came blobby fish-like things that swam about for a bit until they got cramp and went on land for a bit of relaxation. Then they turned into things with legs, too many legs. Then they lost legs in the war or something and turned into monkeys (still following? This is Darwinism people, keep up!). When the monkeys discovered social awkwardness human beings came into existence and it's been a pretty much downhill ever since.

Humans have reached a point of evolutionary apathy where instead of growing a third leg or an orifice that seeps milkshakes, we just fall off chairs and get hit by cars.

So, what's the next step? Well, I believe the next stage will divide humanity in two. Stay with me on this, I am serious. On one side we will have the 'spheres'. The spheres are gigantic masses of meat with brains that roll around the earth searching for wine and plants. On the other side will simply be clouds of pure energy that have left behind their physical bodies to enlighten their collective knowledge and become one with the universe. I WILL BE A SPHERE. Fuck the energy-cloud thing! I will roll from one Greggs to another, consuming pastries until the universe makes sense.

If you have been affected by any of the issues in this chapter, please see a therapist because there is no one else to help you.

THE TIMELINE OF HUMAN KIND

200,000 BC
People happen, unfortunately

150,000 BC
First hat invented

130,000 BC
Madonna releases her
first single

120,000 BC
Humans discover hummus.
Thousands of years are lost

3,500 BC
Some twats called Adam
and Eve get shitfaced in an
orchard and make up a load
of stories

33 BC
Bruce Forsyth is born

0 BC
Bloke claiming to be son
of God effectively fucks up
the entire world

33 AD
Son of God murdered by
early Italian mafia

101 AD
EastEnders first airs in the UK

200 AD–2000 AD
Wars and shit. Like, loads of
wars and shit. Most for no
bloody reason

2015 AD
Everything is just kind
of fucked up

ILLEGAL

Laws put in place to stop you attempting to become a Supervillain.

'If it wasn't for law enforcement and physics I'd be unstoppable' – Unknown

This is very true. Negate the physics part for a moment and focus more on illegal activities. In my hometown of Hereford, it is still legal to kill a Welshman with a crossbow on a Sunday so long as you are in front of the cathedral. It is difficult to believe that this can still be legal but I kick a child on a train who won't stop crying and I GET ARRESTED. It's sick.

Some laws apply to others and not me. I can't get my head around it. You try to become a Marvel Superhero ONE TIME and you get kicked out of B&Q for throwing hammers at the customers. You try to be Doctor Who ONCE and you get arrested for flailing a screwdriver at a young woman in a portaloo. You try to play Quidditch ON ONE

OCCASION and you are put on a register for throwing brooms at children during a sports day. The hypocrisy is ridiculous.

When I inevitably become prime minister, I will make it illegal to push onto trains before other people alight. If you attempt to do this, you will be sentenced to a weekend with THE BEES. This is a simple punishment I will enforce, in which the person found guilty of any heinous crime, littering, not owning a dog, having bad hair, will be subject to. You will be locked, for one weekend, in a room full of bees. That's it. You can bet no one would push past me on the Jubilee line again anytime soon.

A more suitable punishment for criminals would be something so horrific, so embarrassing, that they would never offend again. I am, of course, talking about *deep breath* making them read their internet history to their grandmother. No one would ever commit crimes again if you had to read your YouPorn favourites list to old Mabel.

IMMIGRATION

Selfish bastards trying to find a better life. Gits!

'Look at them lot, coming over here, wanting to take all our low-paid jobs we don't want because we all have degrees in social media. Aren't they just happy in their own country? This is ridiculous, I'm moving to Spain.'

White people get really angry about immigration. It's in our top three favourite things to get angry about, just before parking tickets but after our food being too spicy when we ordered it mild. The thing is, the MASSIVE point that EVERY sod who argues against immigration is that WE ARE ALL IMMIGRANTS. The human race fell out of the sludge and began in Africa. From there we all went weird, built invisible lines between countries and kept shouting 'FUCK OFF' at each other.

I for one was thoroughly disappointed when UKIP shouted that 3m Romanians were coming to England, and none of them turned up. I expected to wake up and find my cupboards filled with Romanians. I try to go to the bathroom: Romanians. I just want to climb a tree — wait, Romanians.

Yes, immigration needs to be regulated, and yes, illegal immigrants are bad, but treating other HUMAN BEINGS as anything less than that simply for wanting the privilege of enjoying the lifestyles we all take for granted is a new sort of madness. They are everywhere. In your schools, their children getting 'educations'. They are in YOUR shops selling YOU food so they can make 'money' and 'feed' their 'families'. Disgusting! Down with this sort of thing.

UK Citizenship test

Home Office

1. What is the national animal of England?
   - A- Bears
   - B- Foxes
   - C- Dragons
   - D- Lions

2. What is the correct response when someone drops a pint in a pub?
   - A- Help them
   - B- Make sure no one is injured
   - C - Shout 'WAHEY' like a dickhead

3. Do you put the milk in your tea first?
   - A - No
   - B - Get the fuck out of this country

4. Please explain the offside rule in 300 words or less.
   ....
   ....
   ....

5. If someone has a cold at work, the correct response is:
   - A- Sympathy
   - B- Hiding
   - C- Saying 'Oh, that's going around at the moment' and walking away.

6. What is the correct spelling?
   - A- Bendybus catflap
   - B- Benedict Flumberclack
   - C- Bliggleforth Carcrash
   - D- All of the above

7. How old is Queen Elizabeth the 2nd?
   - A- 90
   - B- 190
   - C- Immortal

8. Going to Nandos for dinner is called having a '.....' Nandos.
   - A- Cheeky
   - B- Saucy
   - C- Erotic
   - D- Horrific

And here is just another reminder of some of the true British values we wish to instil on our friends from other countries:

- Tutting in queues
- Telling pigeons to fuck off
- Complaining at self-checkout machines
- Being a bit racist
- Making tea wrong
- Complaining about immigration
- Wanting to move to a foreign country
- Only ordering chips when dining abroad
- Talking about the weather
- Never trusting anyone who was famous in the 1970s
- Radio 1 for some fucking reason
- Being surprised *The Daily Mail* are being twats again
- Shouting out of cars at women
- HARD. WORKING. PEOPLES.
- Being afraid to put an England flag in your window in case your neighbours think you're part of the EDL
- Doing a sick in a Wetherspoons
- Having one of the three designated hairstyles
- Being afraid of the Welsh for some reason
- Ducks, everywhere, just ducks
- Actively avoiding ITV
- Apologising to doors, lampposts and other inanimate objects

INSECTS

Legs with things attached to them.

And on the Fifth Day, God got really pissed and stopped giving a shit and created insects. He made them from limbs he had left over from creating other living things and decided to attach them on things that could kill you and definitely annoy the crap out of you.

WASP FACTS

Wasps are the meth addict cousin of bees.
Their only purpose is to ruin picnics and make
men flail around like ballerinas on ketamine.

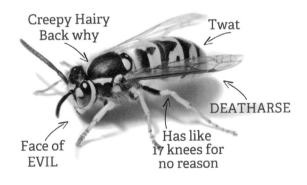

Creepy Hairy
Back why

Twat

Face of
EVIL

Has like
17 knees for
no reason

DEATHARSE

- Wasps feel no remorse
- They can lift 17 times their own weight
- They will try to fly off with your children
- The only way to kill a wasp is to panic
- Wasps can cause rational men to exaggerate

God: 'Ants are weird, aren't they?'
'Don't.'
'I'm going to...'
'Please don't'
'I AM GOING TO GIVE SOME OF THEM WINGS.'
'For the sake of fuck!'

All insects are creepy. There is no situation that can be improved with the addition of a million insects. Unlike how most situations would be improved with the addition of a million puppies, a garden filled with fire ants is much less enjoyable. I understand that bees are a necessity to our fragile ecosystem, but their drunk and violent cousins wasps are just the arthropodic equivalent of that bloke who goes to a Wetherspoons just to start a fight.

There are too many of these creepy crawlies. From worms that are basically inside-out snakes to moths that are just homeless butterflies. And then spiders. Spiders are just gloves that are possessed by Satan. Some spiders can grow as big as a Volvo and will hold your family hostage for days if they can.

QUICK TIP:
Humans will eat eight spiders in their sleep during their life span. Eat them while you're awake and leave carcasses around your bed to show the other spiders you aren't fucking around.

It's creatures like this that make humans never want to leave their house. Inside your home there is internet and cakes. Outside there are flying bastards with needles on their arses and moving hairy Tupperware boxes filled with venom. It's safer inside. OR IS IT?

INTER COURSE (SEXUAL)

The thing your parents did that you never want to talk about.

Ever wonder what position you were conceived in? Does the position you were conceived in affect your personality? Are those who were created in the Missionary more likely to be sensitive, as their parents were making eye contact at the time of their conception? Are those who were brought into being while in a six-way swingers' party more prone to loneliness?

Well, I will let you think about that. OK, horrified enough? Let's continue.

Now, kids, intercourse is where you take your genitals and smack them against a stranger because you make poor life choices.

Eventually you will find someone that you quite like disappointing on a regular basis, then you just watch box sets and wait for death. You get to have sex with as many consenting partners as you want in this life. Some people have sex with only one person their entire life. Some people have sex with more than seven people during the course of their existence, which frankly sounds tiring.

Sex is an intimate moment in life where two, or three, or if you're low on money and trying to get through college, 15 people will come together to make noises on each other for 20 minutes then need a nap. The original purpose of sexual intercourse was to create a baby, but because babies are expensive people have stopped doing that and now prefer to drink a lot and pretend they're happy. The dangers of these liaisons are numerous, but the most important one to be terrified of is catching a disease that will make your undercarriage look like a burst pie for several weeks. Then you have to show your crusty mound to a nurse who will laugh at you until you leave. Remember, always use protection when having sex. Can't afford an entire wetsuit and a mini trampoline? A condom will do just fine.

Intercourse can be a magical event for one or both members of the activity, and should not be engaged in lightly. Don't be forward, don't rush it – it's not a game of pop-up pirate, there are no winners, only losers.

The 'I'm missing my show can we both face this way?'

The 'that was a fantastic six minutes thank you'

The 'what the fuck are you trying to do here?'

The 'Jesus Christ my back'

My knee doesn't go that way

What? Stop making that noise. What is that smell?

The 'This seemed like a good idea at the time and now what the fuck are we doing?'

The Indiana Jones boulder scene

The 'ow get off my hair'

The mid-thrust existential crisis

IKEA disaster

Sliding lap dance

Apathyplank

The Do-It-Yourself

This

JEALOUSY

Looking at someone and thinking… fuck you!

JEALOUSY IS UGLY

JUST LIKE YOUR MUM

YOU CAN'T SPELL JEALOUSY WITHOUT LOUSY OR JEA

JEALOUS MEANS JUST EVERYTHING ABOUT LOVE OVERUSES SCIENCE. WHAT

EMOTIONS ARE LIKE FARTS IN A LIFT. NOBODY WANTS THEM AND BLOODY HELL HOW ARE YOU ALIVE

OK, that's enough of the Facebook-style motivational posters.

I am jealous of many people. I am jealous of attractive people, I am jealous of normal people and I am jealous of dogs. Fluffy gits walking around everywhere being adorable and getting away with anything, must be like being a Royal.

Jealousy, however, is useful to help us strive towards our goals. Without it we would be complacent in our mission to do very little and eat cereal in front of *Antiques Roadshow*. Seeing old friends on Facebook doing better than you is the best way to inspire yourself. 'Chubby Simon from Year 8 just married a Thai millionaire? Yeah, well, today I ate a whole packet of Hobnobs without burping so who is the real winner here?' I say to myself, trying not to allow the jealousy in.

JEALOUSY BECOMES EVEN MORE APPARENT ON SOCIAL MEDIA:
Steve's status 14th June: 'Ran a 5K in 30 mins today, #blessed'
Robert replies to Steve: 'Good work, mate, I can do a 5K in 22 mins, you'll get there!' Fuck off, Robert!

Gemma posts a selfie to Instagram: 'Just finished my eye make-up, J'adore! #Selfie #Me #Lookatmyface #Welcometomyface'
Kim replies: 'Wow, looks nice! What brand is it as I think it'll look much better on me!' Fuck off, Kim!

'Jenny has fed baby Sue today, baby Sue is happy.'
Sarah comments: 'Good work, Jennybabes! I just fed Tomas through his new £50 bottle.'

And so it begins, the Mum-off. The greatest of the social media competitions. One mum has thrown down the gauntlet, who shall win? The mothers argue for hours about how many steps their babies can do, what words they know, what their favourite episode of *Lost* is, until one mother doesn't comment back. The winner pours herself a cup of tea and updates her status: 'Feeling smug.'

Jealousy leads to determination, determination leads to perseverance, perseverance leads to hate, and hate is the path to the dark si... WAIT.

JOBS

Things to discuss with people you don't know at parties.

How many toddlers out there said to their parents, 'When I grow up I want to get a degree in media and then because of the suffering employment market work in a coffee shop until I'm 40 and grow an awful beard'? Maybe some toddlers from Hoxton but they don't count.

When I was little I wanted to be a vet, then I realised that all vets did was kill my pets and that's how I became such a pessimist. You are pressured with what you want to do in life from such a young age. You are made to feel like your life is only meaningful if you are employed. That you live to work, not work to live. In your years of education you should learn that happiness comes first and work second. That complicated equations and religious education mean fuck all when you're scanning the barcode of an orange for the sixteenth time because you don't want to call your supervisor.

The cruellest thing about employment is how your employer values your time. You are literally paid on how much they believe an hour of your life costs. An hour of your life can be worth £6 to one person or £6,000 to someone else. And at the heart of it all they don't care. They can get someone to replace you. YOU, the most important person in the world, are replaceable. No wonder thousands of us call in sick each week just so we can sit at home in the dark and THAT feels more reasonable.

Getting a job in this market is horrific, but don't let anyone undervalue you: they need YOU. And you are FUCKING AWESOME... OK, maybe not that great, you've got a bit of stuff on your cheek, it's... no, left.... OK, you got it!

How To Survive A Work Day

Gym

Go to the gym before work so that one day you will be strong enough to fight your boss.

Commuting

To get yourself in the right frame of mind for work listen to really sad music on your commute and reflect on all the bad choices you have made in your life.

Get to work early

If you get to work first you can hide in the cupboard and scare the shit out of Linda from Accounts.

Time Management

Divide every hour into 20-minute segments, the average length of an episode of The Simpsons. Now there's only four episodes til lunch!

Email

If anyone says they are going to 'ping' you an email, you are legally allowed to challenge them to a duel.

Joy

A feeling of elation usually caused by happiness or when you see free food at work.

People find joy in different places. For some, it's in the smile of a newborn baby's face, for others it's lederhosen-themed cocaine sex orgy.

Is it harder to find moments of joy in today's busy world? Is it easy to turn off your mind when life is a myriad of debt, work and 2am fried chicken? Perhaps joy for you is settling in your lover's arms at the end of a hectic day, perhaps it's swearing at people on the internet as your fedora slowly assimilates into your head. However you find your joy (as long as it's legal... I'm watching you), you need to make time for it.

As a depressive (HA! Thought you were going to make it through a chapter without me bringing that up, did you? NO SUCH LUCK) finding joy in the day-to-day can be a difficult if not impossible task. Watching people with their cheery dispositions evokes envy, jealousy and maybe hunger if it's about lunchtime, but the last one might be time specific.

The very idea of joy is something that we take for granted. We cocoon ourselves in THINGS and PEOPLE and try to ignore the misery in the world. Now, so that this doesn't end up sounding like an essay written by a 14-year-old English student, here are some quick ways to cheer yourself up if you are ever at home and feeling down:

Pretend it's the 1990s by going to the bathroom and reading the back of a shampoo bottle.

Pretend you are an award-winning actor by holding an Action Man and hysterically telling your parents you love them.

Pretend you're sleeping inside a Tauntaun, like Han in *The Empire Strikes Back,* by filling your sleeping bag full of mince.

Pretend you're taking the entrance exam for Hogwarts by talking to yourself while wearing a hat.

PRETEND YOU'RE A FLY BY GOING INTO ROOMS NO ONE WANTS YOU IN, THEN SPEND HOURS SLAMMING INTO WINDOWS, TRYING TO ESCAPE.

Pretend you're a Page 3 model by telling your family your thoughts on current events with your shirt off.

J✎URNALISM

Getting a story and making sure your opinion is all that matters.

174 DEAD IN AIRLINE TRAGEDY

This is a fairly typical headline, it gives statistics: it gives the notion of terror and catastrophe, and it makes you scared. With British media you will usually get:

TWO BRITONS DEAD IN FOREIGN PLANE DISASTER

This lets us know that we should give a shit about at least two of these people, and that it was not a British craft, and that we can blame other countries because as Brits, this is one of our favourite things to do. Then you move onto:

Pilot of doomed plane was a sex-crazed neo-Nazi with three legs and a tail

The tabloid attempt to demonise a human being, as it is so much simpler to blame a single person than a corporation. Plus some secrets about their past are always a way of selling papers. 'Sex-crazed' can refer to that one time they watched porn. 'Neo-Nazi' can refer to the time they accidentally joined a white supremacy rally while looking for a sandwich shop.

16 WAYS TO AVOID DYING ON PLANES

Clickbait. You didn't know there were 16 ways to avoid death, did you? They probably include a funny gif of a monkey in a toy helicopter or some other bollocks.

This footage from the HORRORPLANE will really shock you

I have no doubt that any footage from a disaster will shock me, and I have no intention of watching a recording made in the thralls of terror.

Foreign planes cause cancer and are most likely to not allow us to clone Princess Diana

The Daily Express just putting in their two cents.

News nowadays is essentially one sentence, intriguing enough that you will click through to an article. This article will be laden with adverts, so your click provides the news outlet with money. You clicking on an article about a model's new diet, or a dead baby, pays for more young interns to find images on the internet, so they can keep doing this.

Now that Twitter exists, people can get breaking news on any subject as soon it happens in a 140-word soundbite – with unbiased photos straight from the scene – traditional journalists and news agencies are dying like Arnie at the end of *Terminator 2*. Thumbs up, completely oblivious, but slowly lowering themselves into molten lava. I think that metaphor works. Basically, they're really having to up their game to make sure they are not completely redundant.

Non-Twitter news today is essentially one sentence – a headline – intriguing enough that you click through to the article. The article will be laden with adverts and this provides the news outlet with enough money to buy lunches for the 23-year-old unpaid interns searching for images.

TWENTY THINGS YOU DIDN'T KNOW ABOUT THE ARMENIAN GENOCIDE!

HOW TO AVOID FOREIGN CANCER WASPS

THE NEW DIET THAT TURNED A WOMAN INTO A LITERAL BALL OF THEORETICAL ENERGY

IMMIGRANTS MAY HAVE CLONED PRINCESS DIANA TO LOWER HOUSE PRICES

~J

A CELEBRITY DOES A THING THAT A NORMAL HUMAN BEING DOES BUT THIS IS IMPORTANT BECAUSE CELEBRITY

A TORY MP SNORTS CAVIAR OFF AN ASPHYXIATED OCELOT BUT THE REAL PROBLEM IS PEOPLE ON BENEFITS

ETC.

This revolution in news reportage means that more young people are having their voices heard. We now have more than just the opinion of a 50-year-old with a degree in journalism – we have students, bloggers, artists, actors and comedy writers talking about the news from where they're standing. This way we can find arguments we agree with, opinions vastly different to our own, and insights into stories from every aspect of our culture. However, one rule is still clear... don't read the comments!

KARMA

How the Universe tells you that you are a git.

Karma, Fate, Destiny, these are lovely little lies we like to tell ourselves so that we have something cosmic to blame for when everything goes tits up. A belief in some form of cosmic justice allows us to be unregrettable in our daily actions because we are all selfish and awful.

Does being mean to someone, or doing something unsavoury mean that you yourself are destined for bad luck to fall upon you? Well, for example, we sent a man out to punch toddlers in the face and he got arrested in 15 minutes. Karma. We sent another man out to give sweets to toddlers. He was arrested as well but... OK, this test may not have been the best way to figure out if Karma is real.

It's a great idea, though; you do something decent, then you get something decent in return. It's emotional blackmail to try and trick people into not being complete fucktrumpets for once in their lives. It's the same thing they teach children: don't be a little shit in school and you'll get dinner tonight, be a prick and we'll lock you under the stairs until you're 11. OK, that's Harry Potter. This chapter has really gone to shit, hasn't it?

BASICALLY if you need to believe that the Universe is going to kick your ass if you do something bad instead of thinking that doing something bad is probably just a bad thing to do, you're an asshole. Bad things probably happen to you because you are an awful excuse for a human being in general, not because you didn't separate the glass and plastic in the recycling.

Does Karma exist?

What you do	What Karma will give you
Punch a cat	Get attacked by a lion
Be mean to a friend	Fall down a manhole
Give money to charity	Unlimited blow jobs
Help an old lady cross the road	Unlimited blow jobs
Not kick a child that is in the way	Not get put on a register
Tell people how they are wrong on the internet	Infinite swag and adoration from all women ever
Eat the last After Eight	Go straight to hell, do not pass go, do not collect £200

KEBABS

A box filled with some green stuff, some pink stuff and oh God, what is that?

Eating while drunk is an art. Depending on your wallet it can be a banquet or a pauper's meal.

I have, unashamedly, while rather broke, eaten an entire pack of chicken dippers with a pot of Marmite at 3am. I have accidentally made olive oil on toast. I have eaten half a loaf of bread with gravy. When drunk, I'm a culinary genius.

If you are on the street upon your journey to your home, your feet going in separate directions, your body slowly rejecting you, you can find the worst food ever conceived for cheap. Fried 'chicken' (could possibly be pigeon, seagull, magpie) in enough mayonnaise to drown an otter. You can get chips with the consistency of week-old pasta. A pizza like a frisbee covered in Cheesestrings. A burger like a foot between two drinks coasters. The choice is endless.

But, the kebab. The kebab is something you can only buy correctly in Britain. It is a large lump of congealed animal spinning in front of a radiator, sweating as you stare at it. The dejected person behind the bulletproof counter uses an ice scraper to remove the outer layer of the hairy turning mess. It is then placed with lettuce and a sauce thick enough to remove hair from a plughole. When you eat it, you can hear your cells dying. You hair turns white and you become a being of existential light who will awake in front of a toilet at 8am... and you know you have a meeting at nine.

KEBABS

All kebab meat is sourced locally. Mostly from bins, but still locally.

Mystery Kebab
Six sheets of mystery meat layered with some green shit and a sauce that smells a bit like a discharge.

Lamb Kebab
(No actual lamb is used in this kebab) Comes with chips!

Donna Kebab
We don't know who Donna is or what she did to deserve ending up in a kebab but it's not that shit-tasting.

STEAK & CHIPS

No one has ever ordered this

SOUTHERN FRIED CHICKEN

'Chicken' 2 pieces for £2 or 5 pieces for £6. No refunds if you find a beak or a horn.

KIDS MEAL

Made from real baby goats, comes with chips and 'salad'.

BURGERS

Basic Burger
Everything in the shop chucked between something resembling bread.

FISH & CHIPS

I wouldn't if I was you.

STARTERS

Hummus OR some chicken finger things or more hummus.

EXTRAS

Chips
Soggier chips
What we found downstairs
Growling cabbage
Fuck, the cabbage is loose!

CHIPS

CHIPS CHIPS CHIPS CHIPS
CHIPS CHIPS CHIPS CHIPS

DRINKS & SWEETS

Coke no, is Pepsi OK?

KIDS

Something that screams in supermarkets after two people smash their genitals together.

When a young couple get tired of being mild alcoholics, they tend to change their Facebook status from 'So hungover lol' to 'WE ARE HAVING A BABY'. There are two kinds of parent in the digital age. Those who inform you they have chosen to procreate, then just get on with it, and those who must let EVERY SINGLE PERSON EVER know they are spawning midgets. It becomes their everything. The person you knew who you got drunk with, who vomited in the gutter, is now dead: they are now a parent. They post pictures of their crotchspawn constantly. They find sick and poo cute. They are mad! For the same cost as raising a child you could buy 454,000 GOLDEN RETRIEVERS. HOW IS THIS EVEN A DECISION?

When baby animals are born in the wild, in their first few days of existence they have to avoid predators, survive the elements, find food and build a house, probably. Human babies are USELESS. They don't pay taxes, they can't pick a good wine, they refuse to speak English... Frankly, it's insulting.

Then there is the sordid business of forcing this creature into the world. Women go through hours, weeks, months of pain, men just... provide biscuits. THEN PEOPLE DO IT AGAIN. A thing forces its way out of your body, drains your life force, takes your money and becomes slightly hairier, AND PEOPLE DO IT AGAIN.

How babies are made:

When a man and a woman meet at a bar and have a few drinks, they go home and make disgusting noises on either other for 20 minutes.

Then after several arguments and 9 months, a drunk midget with no personal boundaries explodes out of the woman and starts getting into debt the end.

Having a baby vs having a framed picture of Christopher Walken	Baby	Christopher Walken
Costs loads of money	✓	✗
Poops everywhere	✓	✗
Means you can't go out	✓	✗
Annoys your friends	✓	✗
Cries in pubs	✓	✗
Needs entertaining	✓	✗
Is AWESOME	✗	✓

KIN

A group of people you are legally forced to argue with.

You only get one family. Unless you are a Mormon, or remarry, or steal children. OK, FINE, but you only get one set of parents. Unless your parents question their sexuality after your birth and marry. FUCK'S SAKE, OK!

Family are a bunch of weirdos you wouldn't usually associate with in your normal social circle. They inform you when you've gained weight, tell you when your hair is shit and ask how your failing job is going.

Your parents' job in this world is to make you the best person you can be. However, this job is slightly difficult when they are also programmed to allow you to express your own unique identity between the ages of 13-19, usually where you end up with long hair, a hemp hoodie and smell like a geography teacher's car most of the time. You argue, then when you get to your mid-twenties you just get drunk with them at weekends.

Siblings are friends you are forced to hang out with. As you grow up, this becomes easier and the random beatings dissipate, and you usually find out you hate the same things.

Cousins are siblings you don't see very often, who are doing much better than you in life and your parents don't refrain from reminding you of this.

Aunts and uncles are parents who have little power over you yet still scare you for some reason.

Grandparents are cool as fuck because they know they can get away with spoiling you, and in a few hours just hand you back to your parents, stuffed with chocolate or whisky, hyperactive and loud, and it's not their problem.

Godparents are people your parents tell you about but you are almost positive they don't exist as you have never met them.

Family is important. Your family will always love you, unless you're a prick. Yes, you argue, yes, you scream at each other and no one is good at making any decisions, but tell your people you love them because they have always been there for you, and I am sure if you need them right now, they will pick up the phone.

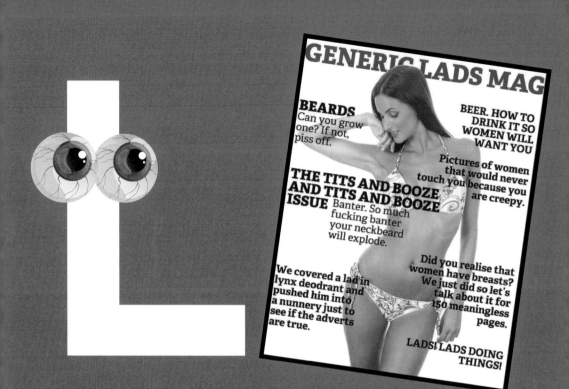

LAD

A type of man who needs to be set on fire.

'Boys will be boys' is the worst excuse for dickish behaviour around. Lad culture perpetuates the ideal that young men can be loud, obnoxious, vile and self-important, and gives them an easy way to get out of most situations they put themselves in. To become a proper LAD, you must first obtain a purely objectified opinion on women. Shouting at them out of vans, using your entitlement to thrust yourself into their personal space, and dismissing their repulsion at your advances with verbal and personal attacks.

[PLEASE READ THE FOLLOWING PARAGRAPHS IN THE VOICE OF DAVID ATTENBOROUGH]

The average lad enjoys taking his shirt off upon the beam of sunshine of the year. They enjoy cheap beer on trains, shouting at pigeons and discussing that game where attractive men in tight shirts run about after a ball, yet they still use the word 'gay' as an insult.

They can be found gathering in Wetherspoons on a Friday night, attempting to attract a mate with the scent of Lynx deodorant and a plumage of polo T-shirts in bright colours. Their main language derives from English, yet words such as 'banter' and 'tits' are three quarters of their vocabulary, the other quarter being replaced with grunting sounds. They find James Corden funny, they enjoy the music of Mumford & Sons... They need to be stopped.

What is a LAD?
Mostly bloody awful, to be honest

Gormless fucking expression
(The average lad can only process six thoughts a day)

Snapback cap with label still attached
(The label is kept on as a sign of dominance)

Awful taste in beer
(It is rumoured that if a Lad drinks ale he could die)

Tribal Tattoo
(Despite never actually being a member of a tribe... Just another lie)

Arse hanging out
(Much like baboons, lads keep their arses hanging out like a ham sticking out of a pile of laundry)

Jogging bottoms
(These are a common form of attire for the lad. They will be worn to the pub, job interviews and funerals.)

Expensive Trainers
(the only thing they will spend money on, for some fucking reason)

LANDLRDS

*Rich people who buy one-bed houses
to turn into 1,700 studio flats.*

HOW TO RENT A FLAT IN LONDON:
Step 1: Begin search
Step 2: Search for two months and look at some of the worst places
      humans could possibly live
Step 3: Cry
Step 4: Go back to Step 1.

A one-bedroom flat in London costs approximately the same amount
per month as a pop star's cocaine habit, a castle in Scotland or the
down payment on a superyacht. All flats come with a bit of ceiling
that winks at you, taps that designate their own temperature and a
shower that give the experience of being urinated on by a elderly
squirrel with a prostate problem.

    Why does living in London cost three times more than other
places in the UK? The wages are slightly higher to compensate for
the expense of being alive in this city. It is important to cram enough
people into Zones 1–2 as humanly possible, so cupboards, sock
drawers and tobacco tins are sold as student accommodation.

    Estate agents are men and women that, several years ago, traded
their souls to Satan for a night out in the city, and their penance is
to be given one single haircut between them and be forced to lie
about property. Landlords, on the other hand, are people who prey
on the lower and middle classes. Often living abroad as they have

grown tired of Britain, but leaving a run-down house somewhere on the M25 to be sold by estate agents to desperate young people attempting to gain a career in media.

This year, rent increased with inflation, however, the size of my flat did not increase. So I began spending more money on the same floor space and the pet mould growing in the bathroom corner. Until this mould starts paying rent, I will continue to put it down as a dependent on my tax returns.

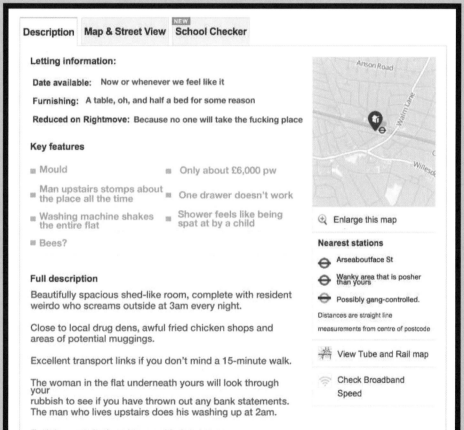

Description **Map & Street View** **NEW** **School Checker**

Letting information:

Date available: Now or whenever we feel like it

Furnishing: A table, oh, and half a bed for some reason

Reduced on Rightmove: Because no one will take the fucking place

Key features

- Mould
- Only about £6,000 pw
- Man upstairs stomps about the place all the time
- One drawer doesn't work
- Washing machine shakes the entire flat
- Shower feels like being spat at by a child
- Bees?

Full description

Beautifully spacious shed-like room, complete with resident weirdo who screams outside at 3am every night.

Close to local drug dens, awful fried chicken shops and areas of potential muggings.

Excellent transport links if you don't mind a 15-minute walk.

The woman in the flat underneath yours will look through your rubbish to see if you have thrown out any bank statements. The man who lives upstairs does his washing up at 2am.

Fuck knows what's going on with the shower.

Anson Road

Walm Lane

Willesd

Enlarge this map

Nearest stations

Arseaboutface St

Wanky area that is posher than yours

Possibly gang-controlled.

Distances are straight line measurements from centre of postcode

View Tube and Rail map

Check Broadband Speed

*A series of mistakes made in between
being hungover in coffee shops.*

You burst out, you get into debt and you die. The events that occur in between are of your choosing and will usually affect your life in a negative way. As children we learn to hope, as teenagers we learn to despair, and as adults we learn to accept. We grow as people and we try to leave a legacy on this planet that can proudly say, 'I WAS HERE, AND I FUCKED IT UP AS LITTLE AS POSSIBLE'.

What is the meaning of life? To procreate and throw miniature versions of yourself into the world? God no, one of you is enough. To do unto people as you would have them do unto you? Ridiculous! Everyone would just be giving each other blow jobs all the time and nothing would get done. To try and make the world a better place with your presence? You already do, you stay out of the world's affairs, this is the best you can do.

At the very moment you are reading this, 6bn other stories are being made around the world. Six billion people are just trying. The real life lesson everyone should learn, and it is the most important one, is that none of us know what the fuck we are doing. Anyone who does is a bloody liar. They never tell you as a child that when you are an adult you still won't know what the hell is going on. The best you can do from day to day is to try and fuck up as little as possible.

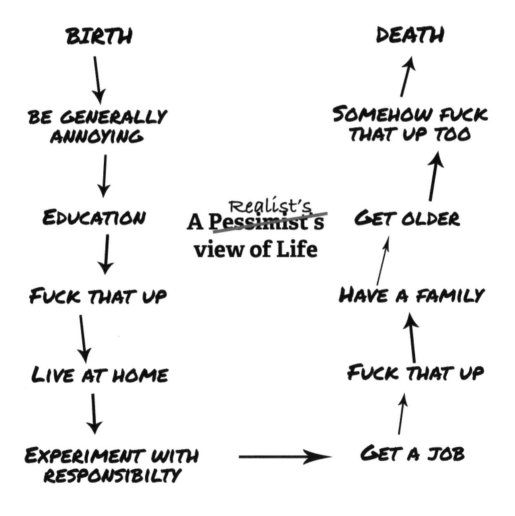

LOVE

Oh, bloody hell!

All everyone wants in life is to find someone who looks at them the way a dog looks at your food.

Poetry is filled with analogies of what love feels like...

Love is like feeling hungry and seeing a packet of Space Raiders on the office desk next to you and your colleague isn't looking.

Being in love feels like starting a new TV show and knowing there are 12 more seasons.

Romance is like spending a few years of your life on an audition for the worst job ever.

Marriage is like a great movie, but it's directed by Sofia Coppola and very little happens.

Finding someone to adore you is the emotional equivalent of finding your keys.

When two people can go around an IKEA store without wanting to murder each other in the most horrible of fashions they are in love. The feeling of murder may be still there, but you probably won't go through with it, because you split the bills now.

You don't choose who you fall in love with, but you should because if you don't choose then you end up with someone bloody awful with back spots and webbed toes. Finding the right person can take a while and you'll think you have fallen in love a couple of times before the BIG ONE. The only advice I can give is that you should find someone who is essentially your best friend, that you can get drunk with a lot, and can be silent around without someone starting A REALLY BORING CONVERSATION. Then when you get bored of being mild alcoholics together you start a family and become interested in gardening and discussing what you're having for dinner in six months' time and it's all quite, quite terrible.

So for you special few, I give you a free sample of my next book entitled 'Love in the Time of Autocorrect'.

LOVE IN THE TIME OF AUTOCORRECT

HE MOVED HIS HAMS UP HER LEGS, HER VOLCANO QUID DITCHED IN ANTICIPATION. HE MOVED HIS LISPS TOWARDS HERS. THEY KISSED. IT WAS A HARD KISS. THEIR TONGS ROAMED LIKE TWO SNEAKERS IN A HEDGE.
'ARE YOU READYSETGO?' HE ASKED SEDUCTIVELY.
'YEMEN,' SHE REPLIED.
HE LOOK OFF HIS SHIRLEY TEMPLE, SHE REMOVED HER TORY LOGO.
HE MALEFICENT BREADS EXPOSED, HE LOOKED STUNNED AS SHE MOVED HOUSE.
THEIR BODIES MOVED AS ONESIES. SWEETS POURED FROM EVERYWHERE.

MAKE-UP

Chemical combinations used on a human face.

Many men believe women wear make-up to impress men. This is in fact a shed of lies. A warehouse of falsities, a bunker or mistruths. OK, I let that get away from me. Men are terribly self-important, so it takes some time to get around the fact that women are doing something that isn't for them. Because, in a man's mind, everything is about them.

Just try and get your head around this... women, women right, women do stuff for themselves. It's ridiculous, isn't it? They want to look nice and feel confident in their beauty. Weirdos! At least we don't live in a world that vindicates women for even the smallest of physical flaws. Men scream, 'this is why I have trust issues!' When they see women without make-up, even though most men smother themselves in a veneer of self-important delusions. If it's not your body, who gives a flying bollock what you do? Your body is your own, you only get one and learning to become comfortable in it can be one of the hardest things we do.

I have lived with a beauty blogger for four years now. I know when to say that her eyeliner looks fierce and when to say that her eyebrow game is on-point. I have also discovered that I look fucking fantastic in make-up, (I say 'fantastic', kind of like Julian Clary after a long weekend on pills) but still fierce. My wife suffers with Rosacea, a skin disorder that leaves her face red, puffy and not to her liking. Make-up and beauty products give her the confidence to go into the outside world and to feel self-assured. It is not for anyone's benefit but hers, and that's how it should be. Life is too short to spend hours making yourself up for other people's opinion. If you feel good in yourself, then do what you need to, to make that happen.

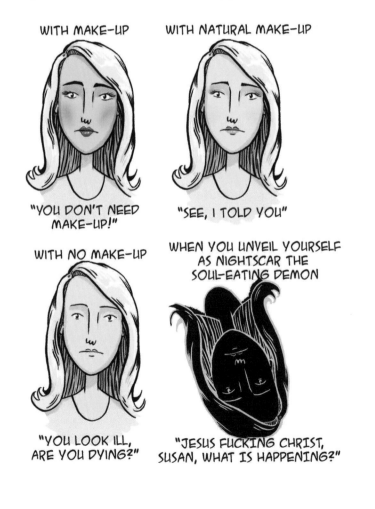

WITH MAKE-UP

"YOU DON'T NEED MAKE-UP!"

WITH NATURAL MAKE-UP

"SEE, I TOLD YOU"

WITH NO MAKE-UP

"YOU LOOK ILL, ARE YOU DYING?"

WHEN YOU UNVEIL YOURSELF AS NIGHTSCAR THE SOUL-EATING DEMON

"JESUS FUCKING CHRIST, SUSAN, WHAT IS HAPPENING?"

MARRIAGE

*The hardcore-boss level
of a relationship.*

Once you have experienced the thrills of the start of a new relationship and you have resigned yourself to the fact that it is very unlikely you will do any better, marriage can happen.

The main point of marriage is a wedding. You get to have a massive party where people come and drink your booze, embarrass themselves and fall over, while you shout from the top of your lungs 'THIS ONE IS MINE, I CLAIM THIS ONE!'

Planning a wedding is like planning a tactical assault on your family. You have to decide where everyone sits (do you sit the left-wing cousin next to the racist auntie just for a laugh?), what food you want (do we prepare steak for all, or save money by just getting Greggs to cater it?) and decide on music for people to dance to (as a tip, nobody dances to 'Bitches Ain't Shit' at a wedding) For the groom, your responsibilities are simple: don't fuck it up. DO NOT. FUCK. IT. UP. Prepare a heartfelt groom's speech and then attend to your partner for the day. My groom's speech looked like this:

And it was fucking brilliant.

Weddings are also so stressful that you require a holiday after the event to recover. While most people envisage a weekend of flailing on each other in a five-star hotel, in reality it is simply a long week where you can read books and respect each other's silence. This is what marriage should be.

WEDDING SPEECH

- THANK EVERYONE FOR COMING
- THANK BRIDESMAIDS WITH WORDS LIKE 'WELL HENCH' AND BOOTYLICIOUS
- BILL PULLMAN'S SPEECH FROM INDEPEDENCE DAY FUCK YEAH
- *BREAKDANCE SOLO*
- THANK YOU TO THE BEST MAN, DO SOME SHOTS
- *RELEASE THE OWLS*
- POWERPOINT PRESENTATION OF EARLY SEXTS
- TALK ABOUT LOVE, MAKE PEOPLE CRY (IF THIS DOESN'T WORK, PEPPER SPRAY)
- *FRESH PRINCE OF BEL AIR RAP*
- *KEYBOARD SOLO*
- TOAST TO BRIDE. AND ME. I'M AWESOME
- FINISH BY RAPPING 'NO DIGGITY' FOR 10 MINUTES
- BALLOON DROP
- DROP MIC AND OUT.

MENTAL HEALTH / STIGMA

Cheer the fuck up.

One in four British adults suffers from mental health issues. Living with depression is like living with a room-mate you never agreed to let stay with you but he's been there for four years now. He leaves his sweaty clothes everywhere, fills the sink with dirty dishes and never cleans up after himself. You just try to live your life as well as you can with him in the same house. He plays loud, annoying music until 4am and starts ruining all the things you love, but you just sit there, trying to ignore him until he goes away.

Attitudes towards depression and Mental Health disorders are getting better, but there is still some way to go. MH patients are still vilified and dissected in the media. When Robin Williams passed away due to depression, many commentators asked how he could suffer from the disorder when he had so much money. When Germanwings pilot Andreas Lubitz crashed his commercial airplane into the side of a mountain in the Alps, *The Daily Mail* asked how people with MH issues were allowed to have jobs like this, not singling out the case, but making a blanket assumption about sufferers. Mental illness is individualistic, and it is not a reason to think less of a person or assume that they can't do jobs or have relationships or be valuable members of society. Many people with mental illness function like everyday 'normal' human beings. They just find everything ten times more difficult than others.

It's also about knowing how to be around people with depression; telling them to cheer up is equivalent to telling someone with a broken arm just to stop having a broken arm. 'It's all in your head'... Well, you're not wrong, but you're not exactly helping.

We need to keep talking about it. I find that writing about what is bimbling around in my head helps. If you feel comfortable sharing your thoughts with others, please do. If you don't, then don't. But there are always people to listen. The Blurt Foundation, Mental Health Foundation, mind.org or Time To Change... there are many charities that you can speak to if you need help. You are not broken, you are not alone, you are not going to suffer in silence. This is shit, but you can kick it in the arse and shout, 'Get out of my house, you hairy twat!' (this is a callback to the first paragraph, keep up!) and kick him down the stairs.

MUSIC

And how all music sounds like vowels trapped inside a dishwasher.

The greatest song ever created is 'Merry Go Round' (1968) by Wild Man Fischer. It is a nonsensical barrage of out-of-tune horns with a man screaming over the top of it. This is when music peaked. Syd Barrett's random attempts at music on his album *Opel* (1988) come a close second, with John Cage's 4'35" coming third.

Pop music is easy to write. First, break up with someone. Then, get a thumping kick drum, a synth keyboard and another singer to repeat every last word of the sentence. Congratulations, you have a platinum record and you get to fall over at awards shows for the next two years before disappearing into the vaults of 'classic pop'.

The main problem with popular music is that it's pop. People don't like popular things. People want to like things they can smugly tell their friends they have discovered, as if they are the only person in the universe listening to this one band.

'Do you like the new Taylor Swift song?'

'Not really, I have been listening to a lot of Bulgarian trance-based beat poetry at the moment. You probably haven't heard of it, it's only big in one pub in Croydon on the 14th Wednesday of the month.'

A QUICK TIP:

If anyone ever says to you, 'God, this is just noise, isn't it?' when you are listening to one of your favourite bands, force them to listen to

122

one minute of any Venetian Snares song. They will never complain that your music is 'just noise' ever again, and also it works as a free laxative.

A QUICK TIP 2:

If you ever want to get a REAL review of an album, simply use *The Guardian* comments section for a free pompous review.

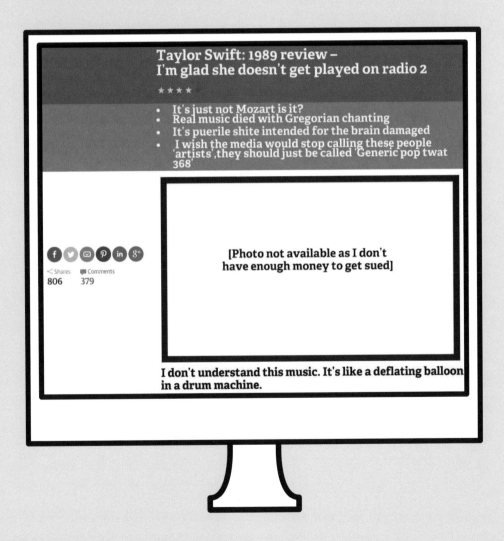

Taylor Swift: 1989 review –
I'm glad she doesn't get played on radio 2

★ ★ ★ ★

- It's just not Mozart is it?
- Real music died with Gregorian chanting
- It's puerile shite intended for the brain damaged
- I wish the media would stop calling these people 'artists', they should just be called 'Generic pop twat 368'

[Photo not available as I don't have enough money to get sued]

Shares Comments
806   379

I don't understand this music. It's like a deflating balloon in a drum machine.

NARCISSISM

Realising that your face isn't the ham balloon
you think it is.

Loving yourself is nothing to be ashamed of. More people should love themselves. Accepting the way you look and being proud of that is quite an achievement today. People will label it as arrogance, vanity and narcissism, but it's simply self-confidence. If more young people were confident in themselves we would have less fan fiction and angsty poetry on the internet, and that could save lives. LITERALLY TENS OF LIVES.

The problem, and yes, there is ALWAYS a problem, is that narcissism can lead to obsession. The obsession to feel validated by your peers. The need to be loved, to be adored and complimented. And this can lead to situations where you become unhappy in yourself. That you feel like you can do better, that you need to be perfect. And that's when the surgery starts, and the new teeth that look like a horse's mouth on a rabbit, the new forehead that can't move, the cheeks that look like a squirrel's preparing for winter... What was once you, the true version of you, is now more resemblant of a melted handbag. You look more like a *Fraggle Rock* character than a human being. And you can't cry about how shit you look because your face is fixed in place like a Madame Tussauds' waxwork after being fire damaged.

If you ever want to feel horrified by your own reflection, simply open your front-facing camera when you are least expecting it. No one, not one single person on this earth, looks good in the front-facing camera from below. We all look like distorted faces sat atop an exploded sausage.

It's not just physical narcissism either, it's intellectual. Every single person on the internet thinks they are the ONLY correct person out there. And they must tell everyone. And how do they do this? The comments section. The comments section is where arguments go to die.

Choose the perfect Social Network for you!

NETFLIX

A way of losing days of your life without having to take drugs.

Settle down, children, let me tell you a tale. A tale of woe and horror. A story of grief in an ancient land. Once upon a time, there was a shop. Not just any shop, because you rarely bought anything. You would use your hard-earned currency to borrow something. The Devil's library. This forgotten place was named Blockbuster.

Unlike today, where you could mash a few buttons and watch whatever piece of media you desired, Blockbuster stood a good half an hour drive away from your house. As with comic book stores, guitar shops and music emporiums, the goblins who worked behind the counter arrogantly thought they knew more than you. You would trek for literally minutes through the winding aisles of B-movies, softcore pornography and Bulgarian documentaries before you would find the newly released section. Then, THEN, you would discover there were no copies left. Nothing can describe the pain, the torment, of wanting to rent *Independence Day* but having to leave with *The Land Before Time 6*.

There is some truth in the whole 'Kids don't know how lucky they have it these days'. You haven't truly lived until you've been in a full-blown argument with your partner in the middle of the Romance section, screaming at each other that it would just be easier to buy *Bridget Jones* than to have to rent it for a sixth time.

But now we have streaming services. Literally, all your favourite

movie sequels kept in one place. You want to watch *Spider-Man*?
Well, you can't watch that but how about *Spider-Man 3*? Or
Spider-Man: The Animated Series? And once you have completed
watching your movie, the site will suggest more things to convince
you not to go outside. 'You've just finished watching *Homeward
Bound*, you might like *The Human Centipede 2*'.

And then of course, there is the Screen of Shame.

"Are you still watching this TV show? You've been
here for 5 hours. You are covered in crisps. Look
at yourself for god's sake"

Continue watching

Back

NORMALITY

We are all special snowflakes, but the snowflakes are MELTING and BASICALLY SLUDGE NOW.

Very few people are normal. 'Normal' is a term used by people who live in three-bedroom houses with a conservatory, have a cat and wear beige trousers. They eat vegetables for fun and watch *A Question of Sport* without vomiting blood. They holiday in Spain every year, and have done so for 40 years. They drink wine in a pub. They listen to Ed Sheeran.

Being told you are not normal is one of the finest compliments you can receive. Even uniformed individuality is better than normality. Have you ever met a normal person? It's like speaking to someone made of Evian.

But one day you can wake up and you've become normal. You go to garden centres on the weekend for fun. Your days of getting smashed and listening to free-form jazz in a dirty basement while misplacing your trousers are behind you. You read *The Guardian*.

Being on the fringe of society has become a badge of honour. You don't have to be what everyone else thinks you should be, you can simply be YOU. Most of your teenage life is spent listening to others tell you how to dress or what to do. So you want to pierce your eyes? DO IT. You want to get a tattoo of John Virgo's face on your chest? DO IT. You want to wear tracksuit bottoms to the supermarket? DON'T DO IT. That's awful. Stop doing that immediately. Go home and put some proper trousers on, good lord!

As my final piece of evidence in the case that 'Being normal is AWFUL' I submit to you, the reader, the day planner of a normal person.

A Day In The Life Of A Normal Person

06	00	Wake up
	30	Stare into the abyss
07	00	Make a cup of tea with no sugar
	30	Listen to Radio 2
08	00	Fetch a copy of The Times
	30	Write a letter to The Times
09	00	Feel smug
	30	Another cup of Tea
10	00	Watch repeats of Countdown
	30	Wonder where life went so wrong
11	00	Start Gardening
	30	Continue Gardening
12	00	God, gardening is shit
	30	I hate Gardening
13	00	Another cup of tea
	30	Go on the internet and watch straight porn
14	00	Research soundtrack used in porn
	30	Contemplate life
15	00	Eat a ham sandwich
	30	Read a copy of Horse Monthly
16	00	Go for a drive
	30	Who the fuck goes for a drive?
17	00	Get home
	30	Take socks off
18	00	Watch Eggheads
	30	Dinner, a single boiled beetroot
19	00	Call ex wife
	30	More porn
20	00	Whisky
	30	Blast some rave music

NUDITY

*A human state only observed during bathing
or when disappointing someone.*

Nudity is nothing to be ashamed of. If I was a woman I would spend most of my time jumping up and down in front of a mirror and auditioning to be one of the Suicide Girls. But there are times nudity is inappropriate: funerals, for example, or taking your shirt off in the park, or willycoptering at your graduation. Society has yet to come to terms with a congratulatory willycopter.

The human body is a bizarre experiment that got out of hand. Hair started appearing in places no hair was supposed to grow. Over the decades the human form came to resemble that of an overpacked sausage covered in rashes. One day I will be attractive, and on that day I will run nude through Whitehall, singing 'Shake It Off' by Taylor Swift. But until that day my mecks (Moob pecks) and keg will stay covered up like a child at a BBC DJ reunion.

The penis is an ugly thing. There are few good-looking penises. Most look like something a forensic scientist would pull out of a horse explosion. Men spend their entire lives priding themselves on their trouser chorizo, using any opportunity to send a picture of it to people on the internet. What angles are best to view it at? The side shot, where it looks like a sad elephant's face? The top shot, where it resembles a dehydrated mole rat? The upshot, where it is the visual equivalent of a butcher's reject bin? Most of the time they just look like thumbs sticking out of a hedge.

When God, or whoever, was creating the human form, She obviously spent the most time on the female, creating a thing of pure beauty, a shining beacon of excellence to determine the human race, then with the bits left over from creating woman, She took a blank mannequin and chucked a mess between the legs.

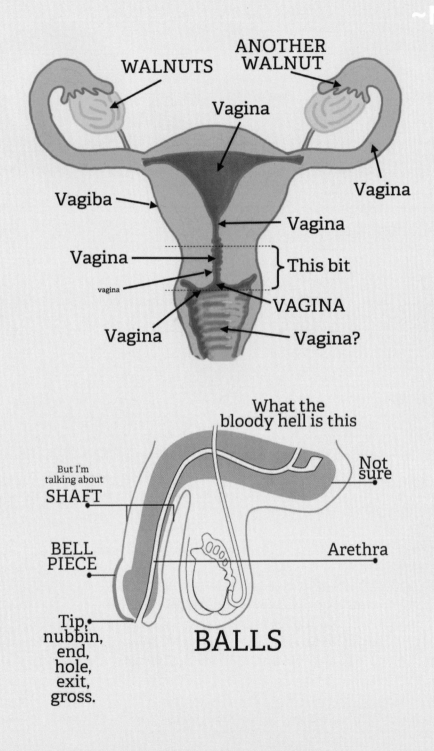

OLYMPICS

*Sports that aren't interesting enough
for an annual event.*

When the Olympics came to London, the city became a nice place to live. Everyone was happy, everyone was cheering and glad to be part of an international event. The main reason London was so beautiful during this time is because all the miserable Londoners had fucked off for a month. The middle to upper classes ran to their country townhouses to fetch polecats and chase the poor or whatever white British people do in the countryside.

The Opening Ceremony approached amid a chorus of 'Holy shit, this will be awful!' And then it came, and the nation stood up and cheered. We had never been this proud to be British. We celebrated our multiculturality, our NHS and our determination, and then the Olympics finished and we all started hating each other again.

The Games themselves were majestic. A nation of people gobbling chips watched as people attractive enough to be pornstars took part in sports a drunken wizard must have invented. At what stage in your life do you discover the one thing, the ONE thing in this world, that you are excellent at, is using a wobbly stick to jump over a six-foot-high limbo pole? What events must occur in your life to force you to realise that you can throw a heavy frisbee further than most people can? And at which point of human evolution, during our millennia of taming horses and riding them into battle, did we think it would be a good idea to teach them how to dance? If I have learnt anything from *Footloose* it's that dancing should be banned, or it causes rebellion. And the Horse Rebellion is coming, my friend. You'll see. You'll all see. If you can't identify the sports of the Olympics by the TINY THUMBNAILS, here is a quick guide:

Extreme Pointing	Fly Twatting	Ball Hoop	Intense Egg and Spoon	Spider Fighting
Tree Removal	Tron	Yoga and falling over	Left Horse	This Way
Floor Tennis	Stick	Professional Clumsiness	Ball Lunge	Git Topple
Fucking Everything	Sparklers	Escape	Battle Egg	Competitive Sitting
Owl Hunting	Testicle Retrieval	Splash	What	Fly Swatting
Genital Wafting	Wasp Cricket	Flee	This	Chase Your Bike

OPINIONS

Incorrect things other people believe.

Opinions are like arseholes: mine is fantastic but yours is bloody awful and please stop showing it to people at dinner parties.

Everyone is entitled to their own opinion: it's called 'freedom of speech'. Still, some people need to realise that their opinions are wrong and it is, in fact, *you* who is correct about everything. Freedom of speech is great – you can call the Queen a chode, you can draw a picture of David Cameron sodomising the poor and you can blog about how much you fucking hate Marmite. Fine. It's when the line between freedom of speech and common fucking sense blurs that problems arise. So many people use the excuse of free speech just to be a complete cunt and piss people off. Yes, you CAN say these things, but you DON'T have to. You could just be nice and courteous to other people's... oh wait, you're painting the Prophet Muhammad in the snow with your urine. OK!

We are all supposed to think individually, we are all supposed to be unique, however, just because you can do something doesn't mean you HAVE to do it.

SOME COMMON OPINIONS THAT ARE COMPLETE BOLLOCKS:

Cheese is nice.
James Corden is funny.
David Cameron doesn't look like a pillow case filled with mince.
Music festivals are enjoyable weekends.

With the freedom of blogging, you now have access to thousands of other people's ideals. You can scrutinise other people's ideologies and leave a comment informing them of all the ways they are incorrect, usually resulting in comments about their appearance or their stupid moustache. Debate is healthy, differing mindsets are required to form a sensible point of view, yet 99% of retorts in debates are YOUR MUM. (I knew I could get another 'your mum' joke in here somewhere.)

Should I put my opinion on the internet?

ARE YOU JUST TRYING TO PISS PEOPLE OFF?

☐ Yes

☐ Mostly

HAVE YOU RESEARCHED YOUR OPINION OR ARE YOU USING YOUR GUT HERE?

☐ My gut

☐ Fuck you

DO YOU HAVE FACTS TO SUPPORT YOUR ARGUMENT, OR ARE YOU JUST GOING TO SWEAR IN CAPSLOCK AT PEOPLE?

☐ I have facts

☐ WHAT THE FUCK DO YOU MEAN, YOU PRICK?

ARE YOU GOING TO BE REASONABLE AND LISTEN TO OTHER SIDES OF THE ARGUMENT?

☐ No

☐ And you can shit off 'n all

IS YOUR OPINION JUST YOU BEING ANGRY BECAUSE YOU ARE BORED ON THE INTERNET AND ACTUALLY QUITE LONELY?

☐ Yes

☐ Mostly

ORGANIC FOOD

Like normal food but more expensive.

Organic food is left to do its thing, hurled out of the ground and thrown at people who wear corduroy at inflated prices. Eating organically has its upsides, obviously: the lack of chemicals in your food means you can smoke and drink a lot more to make up for it. Like most things in life, the actual THING isn't that bad, it's the PEOPLE WHO HAVE ANYTHING TO DO WITH THE THING that are completely awful.

This may be a generalisation, but everyone who actively seeks out organic food looks like a geography teacher at a Grateful Dead concert. But then is it Gluten-Free? Is it Vegan-friendly? Has it been tested on animals? No, no, and yes. These apples have been dipped in gluten, rubbed on a chicken and thrown at a rabbit for several hours before being sold in a market by a man with a moustache resembling burnt pubic hair.

Remember when humans used to hunt giant animals for food? When people would live in caves and wear the skins of their defeated foe for warmth? How old are you? How do you remember this?! Yet now we complain that the thing we are eating didn't have a good life before being murdered to be turned into a kebab. If lambs didn't want to be kebabs, they shouldn't be kebab-shaped. Wait.

There's a better one than that, OK? If fish didn't want to be deep-fried with chips they should evolve to tell us about it. Not just sit there gasping for air like idiots. Animals should be treated fairly, given fag breaks, a comfy house to live in and the best life they can have, before we shoot them up with bolts and turn them into a jalfrezi.

WHAT THE BLOODY HELL IS A CHICKEN NUGGET?
An Investigation

Chicken nuggets are available from anywhere that sells chicken, but what is a nugget? Chickens don't grow nuggets. Are these just chicken testicles?

Where do chicken nuggets come from?
Scientist: We don't know
Which bit of the chicken do they come out of?
Scientist: Yes
You're not answering any of these questions, are you?
Scientist: False
You don't have any idea what a chicken nugget is, do you?
Scientist: Space

As you see, emotional stuff.

OUTDOORS

*A large area filled with things outside
of your control.*

Have you ever been outside? It's basically just Jehovah's Witnesses, wasps and Poundlands. God wouldn't have invented broadband and pornography if She wanted us to go outside and socialise with people. You can now order food to your home, as well as toilet paper and sexual liaisons; if it wasn't for needing to work I would barely leave the house.

The main reason the outside world is awful is because it is full of PEOPLE. People who are not you or your friends or family are people that are not required in your story. They are background characters, NPCs or perhaps one-night stands. That is it. But they are everywhere. The worst part is, some of them want to stab you, they want to rob you, they want to use your skin as the canvas of a Jackson Pollock painting they're making with entrails. But you don't know which one. Which one of these people could be a threat? Best not risk it, to be honest.

Do you know what is truly fucking stupid, though? GUESS. Camping! The sport of ignoring the fact that we now have HOUSES and can BUY THINGS FROM SUPERMARKETS, and sleeping in a sweaty, uncomfortable cocoon of nonsense in the countryside for a few days... FOR FUN. Some people find this FUN. These people often think vegetables are interesting and that *The Independent* is a serious newspaper. HOWEVER, there is a certain condition that makes a human being want to camp.

There are literally no upsides to camping. You can't go to the bathroom properly. You can't get comfortable. No matter how secure your tent, it will be filled with spiders after five minutes. It just feels like sleeping inside an ewok's scrotum. If you or anyone you know has been affected by camping, please call the police.

1. WHAT IS THIS?

2. WHY IS THERE ONLY 1 OF THIS POLE?

3, OH GOD I BROKE EVERYTHING

4. I NOW HAVE AN IMPRESSIVE CAPE

PEOPLE

Things that get in your way when you go outside.

The general population are bloody awful. They really are, though, aren't they? They leave the keyboard clicks on their phones, they talk during movies, they complain at restaurants... It's amazing we've advanced so far as a species when the main thing the general population do is smell bad and get lost in train stations.

Every single person in the world believes that they are the most important person in the world. They are far too busy to be standing in the same queue as you, they need to overtake you on the motorway because their life is the priority. There are few things in this life that matter, but courtesy is one of them. Are people inherently bad? Yes. Can people be good? Yes, but it only takes one journey on a public bus to realise that humanity needs to be stopped.

Public transport brings out the humanity in everyone. People pick their noses in public and flick it into the ether; some sit there blasting music from their headphones that sounds like a pneumatic hamster banging a typewriter. To bastardise a speech from *Blade Runner*, 'I've... seen things... you people wouldn't believe. Dandruff bits on the shoulder of a commuter; I watched bastards litter in the dark near Trafalgar Square... All those... moments... will be lost, in time, like [chokes up] copies of *The Metro*... on... the tube.'

There are some ways to know which humans are decent, though. And this is by ruling out potential bastards...

- Never trust anyone who is rude to retail or catering staff. They are making minimum wage, the problem you have with them is probably nothing to bloody do with them.
- Never trust anyone who uses the ATM twice. You had your chance, there is a queue – we don't have time for you to check all of your finances.
- Never trust someone who interrupts you mid-conversation. Even if their story is more interesting than yours, there is no need to amplify your self-importance in this way.
- Never trust anyone who plays music from their phone on loudspeaker on public transport. Just. WHY?
- Never trust anyone who is mean to animals, because they are the worst people imaginable.
- Never trust someone who puts the milk in first in tea: this is the behaviour of a potential serial killer.
- Never trust someone who puts their bag on a train seat. Did your bag pay for its own seat? No, then fling your bag up your arse for all I care! I need a seat.
- Never trust someone who saw you in front of them at the bar, but went ahead and ordered before you anyway. There is a special circle of hell for these gits.
- Never trust someone who makes you feel negatively about yourself. There is enough going on in life without some fucktrumpet trying to belittle you.
- Never trust anyone who thought the movie *Avatar* was good: it wasn't. It was seven years long and a dude stuck his dick in a horse's dick at one point. Really.

POLITICS

You don't need a definition here,
it's all fucking dreadful.

ELECTION 2015
Everything is fucked
And if it wasn't shit enough here is Michael fucking Gove

| EXIT POLL | CON | 316 | LAB | 239 | SNP | 58 | LD | 10 |
BBC NEWS 22:08 'LL **BREAKING** THE CONSERVATIVES ARE PREDICTED TO

Politics is an awful business. No matter what you do, you are going to piss someone off. Everyone blames everyone else. When a problem arises, no one takes responsibility and they simply scream at each other like toddlers finding out that Santa isn't real. If you've lived in a house for five years, left the bath tap on and suddenly the bathroom is flooded, you wouldn't scream, 'WELL, THIS IS OBVIOUSLY THE FAULT OF THE LAST OWNERS' because THAT MAKES NO SENSE.

What does a Tory Government Mean for you?

- Lower classes to be killed for sport
- Australian billionaires to dictate policy
- Fox hunting to become mandatory in schools
- NHS to be buried at sea
- Nurses to work 27 days a week
- Zero hour contracts for all
- Food banks to be renamed SHAME MARKETS
- Corporations to pay less tax
- Corporations to do what ever the fuck they want really
- Immigrants to be painted red
- Boris Johnson everywhere, all the time, always
- Scotland to be blown up
- Thatcher to appear on the £10 note
- Thatcher to appear on everything
- 6 mile high Thatcher statue to replace nelson in trafalgar sq
- Landlords to be given cannons
- Tuition fees to be raised to a single kidney per student
- BBC to be catapulted into france
- Minimum wage to be paid in feathers

Conservatives
because fuck you and your family

In this bizarre pantomime of British politics, the Conservative Party are Slytherin, while the Labour Party are Gryffindor, the SNP are Ravenclaw and the Greens are Hufflepuff because they mean well but are fucking useless. We used to have a party called the Lib Dems but they talked themselves out of a job.

We sit in a country in the midst of another Tory government. Our Equalities Minister voted against equal marriage and our Health Minister believes in witchcraft. Labour have their own problems – they need to figure out what they are. Are they the Robin Hood of parties, taking from the rich to give to those living off food banks, or are they moderate, too timid to dip their toes into the left wing of the pool? The Lib Dems are the political equivalent of the uncle you wish wasn't showing up at the party. UKIP are only good for parody and the Greens are too much of a cliché to be taken seriously.

Now, after all that, I should be fair: it is easy to slag off the Tory Party.

Were you expecting a 'but' at the end of that sentence? Because you're not getting one.

However, I implore you to elect me at the next election. Here is my manifesto:

- Hangover sympathy-free on the NHS
- Science to create Dragons
- Michael Gove to be sold for leather
- Dogs literally everywhere
- People who say 'Banter' to be catapulted into Nigel Farage
- *Flintstones*-style cars because why not?
- Free onesies for all giraffes
- Stonehenge to be turned into a giant Tetris game
- Horse to be the new national bird
- Moustache Tax
- Free helicopters for everyone
- Put Princess Diana's brain into a mountain gorilla for a laugh
- Fewer ghosts
- Center Parcs to be used for The Hunger Games
- Sky News to be replaced with a livestream of kittens 24/7
- Build Hogwarts
- Ferrets
- Foxhunts to be turned around so foxes now hunt rich people
- Fewer clouds. No clouds. Some clouds. Not sure about this one yet.
- National sport to be changed to cow rugby.

PORNOGRAPHY

Wrestling but with more bodily fluids and better plot lines.

The worst part about the comedown after an orgasm is opening yours eyes and seeing everyone else on the bus looking at you.

'Get off my hair!' she shouted, sexily.
'My leg doesn't go that way,' he moaned
She grasped his back hair.
He accidentally chinned her in the eye...

If young people are learning about sex via the medium of pornography then the dialogue and direction of these 20-minute humpisodes needs to reflect what sex is really like. With the national curriculum leaving youngsters questioning what sex really is, most young men and women are turning to x-rated websites to get their heads around the mystery of copulation.

Normally, human beings don't reproduce by gangbang schoolgirl orgies. Two girls, one cup is not sanitary advice for foreplay, and that video with the two German priests in the field is better repressed. Pornography does not portray a realistic picture of sex. A young person's first time should be a special and horrifyingly awkward experience, not a gambling venture into the world of anal mishaps. If anything, porn is a brilliant guide for how NOT to do a sex on someone.

FIVE-STEP GUIDE ON WHAT NOT TO DO, FOR MEN

1. Don't whip it out whenever. It's not going to look like it does in the movies, more like a soggy twiglet covered in hair.
2. Don't expect anything from anywhere. EVER. You dick.
3. Don't do the thing they do at the end of porn films, it's not nice. Would you like that done to you? No.
4. Don't try and pick her up. Or do. You'll both end up in hospital but I will find it hilarious.
5. Expect a lot more noises. A LOT MORE. Awful noises. Noises you will hear in the back of your mind forever.

Know Your Porn Acronyms

ATM - Arse to Margate

BBW - Big Bloody Welshman

BBC - Big Black Conservative

BDSM- Bloody Daft Sex Mishaps

DP - Double Perspiration

DILF - Dad I'd Like to Fight

DTF - Down to Friendzone

GFE - Girlfriend Explosion

GILF - Grandma I'd Like to Fondly Embrace

MILF - Mother I'd Like To Funfair

PDA - Public Display of Aardvarks

PORN - Preposterous Overly Written Nonsense

STD - Sexually Transmitted Discography

PUBL C
TRANSPORT

Getting from one place to another while surrounded by Twats.

- When going through ticket gates, wait until the person in front of you is 10 metres away, then forget what you're doing.

- Don't research your journey, stand in front of the signs by the platforms looking lost and basically being in the way.

- Change at Bank station whenever you can, it's the easiest way to change trains.

- Don't wait for people to exit the train before getting on. Panic. Run into the train for no real reason like your life depends on it.

- Stand wherever you want on the escalator, 'stand on the right' is a guide, Londoners are kind forgiving people who will not mind waiting.

- Take your meals with you on the tube, most people love the smell of a McDonalds filling the tube car.

- Whenever possible stand in large groups. Even if you don't know these people, just join a group and look confused.

- The doors are closing, what do you do? THAT'S RIGHT. PANIC. THROW YOURSELF AT THE TRAIN.

- Make sure everyone can hear your headphones, don't be selfish.

@TechnicallyRon

7am. You've yet to inhale your coffee, your body is slowly rejecting you. Your eyes are glazed and your hair is matted. There is a man rubbing up against your back and a rucksack in your face. You are commuting.

A Guide to the London Underground

A busy train is the epitome of all that is wrong in the world. Every annoying thing another human can do is represented here. There's the one woman screaming into her phone. There's a man picking his nose. One woman opens a food container that smells of ancient underwear and hot mayonnaise. A group of young men quaff Carlsberg and debate vaginas or the sport or something. This is humanity. This is why you want to live on a desert island.

What are the other viable options? A taxi? Why don't you just ride your gold-plated horse into work? Cycling? Where every other entity on the road wants to annihilate you? You are trapped: trapped in a life of Oyster cards and bad breath.

You could try the bus, a metal tube filled with reprobates swerving past cyclists. A two-storey DEATH TRAP filled with single mothers and unemployed fathers. The bus is no longer an inanimate object, it is a moving sitcom. It engulfs the people and displays their flaws. People make noises on trains you never thought existed. Snorting noises of thick substances in their nose. Weeping comes from a few rows behind you; a drunken man swills a milk bottle filled with Malibu at you.

I commute while wearing headphones. The ostentatiously loud soundtrack in my ears forces reality into the background. I once commuted without my headphones. All that can be heard is despair. The frequency of regret can be heard by dogs. An American woman starts laughing; it cuts through you like a crowbar through butter.

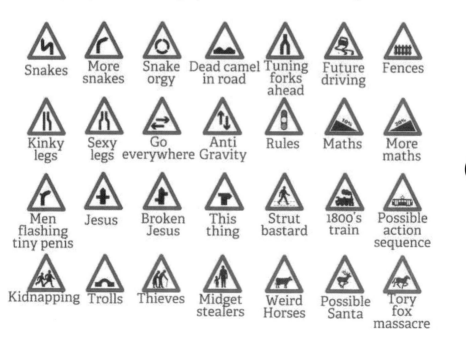

Snakes   More snakes   Snake orgy   Dead camel in road   Tuning forks ahead   Future driving   Fences

Kinky legs   Sexy legs   Go everywhere   Anti Gravity   Rules   Maths   More maths

Men flashing tiny penis   Jesus   Broken Jesus   This thing   Strut bastard   1800's train   Possible action sequence

Kidnapping   Trolls   Thieves   Midget stealers   Weird Horses   Possible Santa   Tory fox massacre

Welcome to the bus, we know it is bloody awful, just stay quiet, keep your head down and don't talk to anyone

 Stop pushing midgets around in buggies. We are on to you.

 No fun please
If you must drink, share with the other passengers

 We are watching you
We can see you reading porn on the top deck. There is just no need for this. Go home and explore your sexuality there.

This scheme is controlled by

Metroline
020 8218 8888

Comments, comp and suggestions

If you have a comment on the service, pleas London Buses
Website   tfl.gov.uk
By phone   0343 222 1234*

If you are not satisfied with London Buses contact London TravelWatch
Website   www.londontravelwatch.org.u
In writing   London TravelWatch, Dexter H
             2 Royal Mint Court, London EC

London TravelWatch will only take up case London Buses have been given the opportu

 **LK12AH**

Assaults
Our staff and passengers have the right to without fear of attack. We will always pre penalties against those who assault.

Travel information
For journey planning, times and fares on al London, please call Transport for London 24 hour Travel Information

 tfl.gov.uk   24 hour travel information
0343 222 1234*

QUEEN (THE)

A pensioner who rules the British Isles
with her army of swans.

I am by no means a royalist; I am a firm believer that the Queen uses her corgis as Horcruxes, eats the souls of the poor and that Prince Philip at some point in his 16 lives was a lizard person. Yet they give a form of comfort to our bizarre, backwards little island. As long as Princess Catherine of Durham or whatever her name is keeps transforming herself into a people cannon every two years, the nation will be able to gather around their television sets and be in awe of a child who, only being four minutes old, already has enough wealth to buy them and their families and force them to perform as jesters in their dystopian kingdom.

The British Royal Family are brilliantly British for a group of inbred Germans. With their massive teeth, their politeness, their ability to eat an ostrich egg in one bite, they are a beacon of aspiration for us poor gutter ferrets living in squalor. Every girl dreams of being a princess, and every boy dreams of being Prince Harry so he can get plastered and not face any ramifications.

Tourism booms in the UK due to the popularity of our German overlords. Millions of uninformed tourists crowd the streets of London for a glimpse of a golden bungalow that got out of hand. I mean, they had to put a theme park in Windsor because there is literally nothing to do there apart from look at some old bricks in a crap formation.

Yet Britain wouldn't be Britain without a 150-year-old Greek man shouting racist slurs at foreign dignitaries.

Identifying The Queen's Horcruxes

Her Majesty is obviously a Dark Wizard. It is important we can identify her Horcruxes.

CROWN
Currently hidden in the depths of Windsor Castle.

Elizabeth the 2nd's earrings
Some say they cannot be destroyed. That they will destroy anyone that comes near them. Prince Philip tried to touch one once, now look at him. He is only 37.

A necklace made from dragon scales.
Can only be destroyed by a virgin.

The Bracelet of Azkaban
Created from the skin of the poor and forged in the heat of the Tory underworld.

NAGINI the Corgi
The most deadly of all Horcruxes.

2 Horcruxes are yet to be found. STAY VIGILANT.

~Q

QUUUUUUEUING
The British National Sport.

To become truly British you must learn some very important things. You must complain about the traffic, even if you were just sat at a traffic light for about 30 seconds. The weather is always the main topic of conversation. If no one has mentioned the weather in five minutes then the conversation is going south. If there is one After Eight left at the end of an evening, insist the other person takes it, then silently seethe with rage as you really did want it.

Being British is a curious thing: we are intrinsically polite, to the point of pain. Yet hidden in this politeness is a contempt for humanity so prevalent that any of us could snap at any time. But us Brits don't snap like normal people snap. We don't show our anger, we merely seethe. We MAY write an angry letter. Or send a subtweet. Or in the most serious of cases, ignore someone for a few days.

The national sports of Britain are queuing, using dogs to mutilate foxes, eating strawberries while two people twat a ball at each other and using umbrellas. That is all we have to offer the world. For a country that once ruled one third of the globe, we can barely make it to work without falling over and trying to sue someone.

British values have been questioned a lot recently. To the right wing, they are a guise for a form of imperialistic wet dream where Britain is somewhere near the Aryan race but with more badger culls. For the left British values mean multiculturalism, sticking out your little finger while drinking tea and drinking ale even though you'd rather have a glass of wine.

But the one thing we Brits do get a bit stabby over is queues. There is a regime here. An unspoken law. We stand, we wait, we use our inner monologues to complain, but this is the way it should be. If you ever cut into a queue in Britain, you will feel the hot painful stare of literally dozens of people. Someone may even tut. If someone in Britain tuts at you, you know you have fucked up colossally.

How to Queue The British Way *(THE CORRECT WAY)*

1. Get to the back of the queue, you prick! You are not the most important person in the world. We are all in a bloody rush. Calm the fuck down!
2. Respect personal space. We all want to get out of here as fast as we can. There is no need to stand so close to anyone that they can smell the egg sandwich on your breath on their neck.
3. DON'T COMPLAIN. We are all very aware that this situation is terrible, but your incessant tutting, cries of 'THIS IS RIDICULOUS!' or general moaning under your breath only make it known to other queuers that you're a complete nob.
4. HAVE YOUR FUCKING PAYMENT READY. We have been in this queue for what feels like six years. How are you still rummaging around in your Mary Poppins' bag for your wallet? Jesus Christ, how are you alive?
5. Do not, DO NOT leave the till to get more shit! You had your chance. You are obviously useless at everything and this should just be a lesson in how awful you are at being a human.

QUINOA

A type of food that SHOULD NOT BE CONSUMED. WHAT IS THIS?

Living in London I have grown accustomed to eating food which is delightfully pretentious. The hipster food movement has hit pubs and restaurants across the capital. The streets are now paved with hummus, your gluten-free, soya latte with extra Himalayan rock sugar only costs the same as a new sofa in a DFS sale. Every burger place is now an artisan beef workshop. The days of a simple meat patty are gone, now you receive a gourmet slab of Hungarian rabbit leg infused with 16 herbs served in a brioche bun with quadruple-cooked potato sticks (chips) served on a wooden board accompanied by a pale ale and you DIE A LITTLE BIT INSIDE.

I don't mind the tiny baskets the chips sometimes come in, or a little pot or something, but when everything comes in its own special receptacle it is no longer a meal, more a do-it-yourself culinary disaster. Plate companies are starting to fold as food is served on chopping boards or in bins, or on the back of a tamed badger. I don't want my pint of beer in a jam jar, it's a needless overcomplication to an already proven method of beverage consumption.

I eat my food so quickly I barely have time to Instagram it. By the time I have got the angle right, the light hitting the baked beans in the right way, the contrast reflecting the struggle of the bacon, the food is fucking cold and I am hungry. I would rather eat my meal, enjoy it and then regale you with a tale of my meal at a later date. Instead of pressing 'like' on your phone, I will come to your house and shout at you about my meal until you make me leave.

London should not be a gourmet bistro heaven. I once saw a man at 3am buy a Chicken Cottage, shout 'CHICKEN COTTAGE!' before being sick outside a Chicken Cottage. That is London; that is real food. You shouldn't have to translate a menu every time you want something to eat.

The Fox and Bollock
Lunch menu

Starters

Sourdough nuggets £5
THIS IS BREAD

Organic garden platter £10
THIS IS JUST A FUCKING SALAD

Chickpea sauce £7
'HUMMUS'

Vegetarian Gourmet Broth £11
SOUP.

Mains

Ground Bors Taurus with Peruvian onion circles smoked sus crofa domesticus and organic lettuce. Served with triple-fried rosemary potato sticks

£20 *A BURGER LITERALLY JUST A BURGER*

Cylindrical Latvian pork wrapped in a homemade pastry, dusted with African fairtrade flour and served with garden greens.

£15 *A SAUSAGE FUCKING ROLL*

A breast of free-range poulet, garnished with bone marrow gravy, roast pommes de terre in oie graisse, land vegetables and risen batter.

THIS IS JUST A ROAST.
£30 *A. ROAST.*

Selected from the finest vache in Bordeux, our Entrecôte is cooked middle to sparce and coated in wild Pacific pepper.

STEAK. BECAUSE STEAK WASN'T **£55** *PRETENTIOUS ENOUGH*

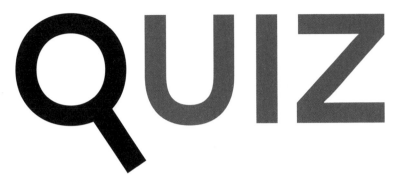

QUIZ ~Q

*Because I am running out of Q's
to write about.*

'And for the next question in this pub quiz, who is the drunken arsehole who keeps shouting out the obviously wrong answers?' 'BARCELONA'

Us Brits love a good quiz. From a question in a Christmas cracker to celebrities embarrassing themselves on *Mastermind*, it's like a drug. The feeling of superiority we gain from getting A SINGLE question on *University Challenge* correct can feed our egos for weeks. Screaming at our televisions because the guy on *Who Wants To Be a Millionaire?* can't get the £500 questions LIKE SOME SORT OF MORON. Our useless bits of trivia give us life. We pray for the moment someone will naturally bring up the Uyghur people of north-west China because then we can regale the group with our ONE anecdote we know about that place, that we only got from an episode of *QI* anyway.

The great British pub quiz. You get a bit drunk, then fall out with all your mates when you realise you are smarter than all of them but they won't listen to you because the bloke with the pen is just trying to show off. You get to invent HILARIOUS quiz-related puns for your team name too! Like 'Quiz on my face', 'Quiz on my tits', 'There's quiz in my eye', 'Fucking hell where is all this quiz coming from... etc', And we've all won a pub quiz once. AND ONLY ONCE. The people who win pub quizzes often are the sort of people who don't leave the house and get mildly aroused by completing a Sudoku puzzle.

CREATE YOUR OWN
UKIP POLICY!

TAKE YOUR BIRTH MONTH

JAN = TAX
FEB = SLANDER
MAR = VINDICATE
APR = TARNISH
MAY = SMEAR
JUN = ANGER

JUL = FUCK
AUG = STOP
SEPT = BELITTLE
OCT = DAMN
NOV = DEFAME
DEC = BOLLOCKS TO

ADD THE WORD THE
AND TAKE YOUR FIRST INITIAL

A = POOR
B = NHS
C = GAYS
D = IMMIGRANTS
E = ELDERLY
F = FRENCH
G = POLISH
H = YOUNG
I = SINGLE MOTHERS
J = DISABLED
K = WORKING CLASS
L = LESBIANS
M = STUDENTS

N = HOMELESS
O = EU
P = SCOTTISH
Q = LIBRARIES
R = NEEDY
S = HELPLESS
T = CHILDREN
U = ILL
V = MIDDLE CLASS
W = FOXES
X = UNEMPLOYED
Y = NURSES
Z = HAPPY

GET YOUR

Daily Mail

NAME

TAKE YOUR FIRST INITIAL

A - CURVY	J - GRITTY	S - BUBBLY
B - SKINNY	K - BLONDE	T - FRUMPY
C - ALL GROWN UP	L - SMUG	U - STEAMY
D - DAZZLING	M - SEXY	V - RACY
E - CREEPY	N - SENSATIONAL	W - DRUNK
F - DISGUSTING	O - PREGNANT	X - CHEEKY
G - BUSTY	P - HALF-NAKED	Y - VILE
H - PERVERTED	Q - ARROGANT	Z - TONED
I - GUILTY	R - PUFFY	

AND TAKE YOUR SECOND INITIAL

A - SCROUNGER	K - BADGER	T - BENEFITS CHEAT
B - IMMIGRANT	L - LANDLORD	U - TEACHER
C - HOMOSEXUAL	M - MP	V - NURSE
D - MUSLIM	N - ENVIRONMEN-TALIST	W - 1970s DJ
E - WOMAN		X - BANKER
F - ROMANIAN	O - TROLL	Y - WORKING CLASS
G - LESBIAN	P - GAY	
H - JIHADI	Q - TAX DODGER	Z - LEFT-WING SCUM
I - TRAITOR	R - FOREIGNER	
J - FEMINIST	S - HOUSEWIFE	

READING

What you are doing right now.
Do I need to explain this? FINE.

Books are like Kindles but with a really long battery life and look better in Instagram photos. Books are read, according to Twitter, exclusively by posh, white men and 20-year-old girls in summer dresses. No one else reads. Ever. Other normal people would stare blankly at a book and wonder how they can access porn on it.

The activity of reading has been around for literally dozens of years. Some books are over ten years old. You get novels, which are like films you have to pay really close attention to. Short stories, like adverts that tell stories, kind of like those John Lewis adverts you get at Christmas time. Poems, which are just random sentences that mean nothing, and plays, which are film scripts performed by people too ugly to be filmed.

The mere concept of reading is bizarre. Every book in the English language is just the same 26 letters used in a different order. A book is an ex- tree, covered in ink, that lets people live another life without having to move. IT'S RIDICULOUS. And, AND, books don't even have to be charged, they don't run out of battery, they don't connect to Wi-Fi. It's just weird.

For those of you just getting into reading, or those of you who wish to re-read some classics from a new point of view, here is my new range of 'Classic books rebranded for Millennials'.

THE GREAT GATSBAE

MOBY DICKPICS

ANIMAL FARMVILLE

GONE WITH THE WINDOWS XP

ONE HUNDRED YEARS
OF SNAPCHAT

THE OLD MAN AND THE BAE

OF MICE AND MENINISTS

A TALE OF TWO TWITTERS

THE TUMBLR OF
MONTE CRISTO

ALICE'S ADVENTURES IN
BANTER LAND

ALL QUIET ON THE WESTERN FONT

HARRY AUTOCORRECT AND
THE PENSIONER OF AZERBAIJAN

A SMARTWATCH ORANGE

THE DM'S OF WRATH

THE PROFILE PICTURES
OF DORIAN GRAY

WUTHERING LIKES

GULLIVER'S TRAVEL BLOGS

LOVE IN THE TIME OF
CANDYCRUSH

BRIDGET JONES'S
LOCKED INSTAGRAM ACCOUNT

CAPTAIN CORELLI'S SYNTH

THE FOLLOWER COUNT
OF THE RING

THE STATUS UPDATES OF
HUCKLEBERRY FINN

THE KINDLE THIEF

THE TIMEHOP'S WIFE

THE FIVE PEOPLE YOU
TAG IN HEAVEN

RELATI♥NSHIPS

The tutorial level of marriage.

How to attract a mate: put on some nice clothes, buy some chips, go to the seaside, wait, that's seagulls. Let's start again.

You see someone in a bar, you find them attractive; they are less ugly than most other people you have been staring at recently. You move towards them, your palms become sweaty, you introduce yourself through a mist of vowels and grunting noises. They offer to purchase your fermented fruit and vegetables on your behalf. Some time later you are lying on top of each other, disappointed but thankful that another human being doesn't mind seeing you naked.

As human beings we are pre-programmed to spend most of our time attempting to find another member of our species with whom to share our lives. Most of this time is spent in regrettable situations with people that we later realise would be more useful for human testing than as prospective mates. Ex-partners provide the checklists by which we define our next victims. 'I liked his penis but his obsession with yodelling at homeless people was really off-putting' or 'His love of literature was insatiable but the fact he was 90% hair and only spoke in rhyme meant my dad would never like him'.

The beginning of a relationship is a competition to see who can get the most friction burn. After you have become tired of changing your bed sheets every day you settle down into the comfortable phase. TV marathons replace sex marathons, stuffing your face with food replaces stuffing your mouth with, well, you know where this is going. After an internal debate about the degree of disappointment their parents may feel upon meeting you, as the current selected human, they decide to let you meet them.

This usually ends horrifically. One parent will call you by the wrong name, usually that of an ex-partner they preferred to you. One parent will ask what you do for a living. Oh God, what *do* you do for a living? Is hobo a job? The first meeting goes terribly; if you are lucky you don't accidentally roundhouse kick your prospective mate in the face.

~R

At the begining of a relationship

I miss you so much

I love you and I can't wait touch you again

I can't believe it's been 10 minutes it feels like years

A few months in

Last night was amazing

I can't wait for tonight :)

A year in

What's for dinner?

Cock

After moving in together

What's for dinner?

Fuck knows what ever is in the fridge that isn't mouldy

After Marriage

What's for dinner?

GOOD GOD I DON'T KNOW

RELAXATION

Trying to feel calm in this
AWFUL WORLD. OH, GOD!

HOW CAN YOU RELAX WHEN THE COUNTRY IS FALLING APART
AND OUR FACIST GOVERNMENT ARE RUINING THE FUTURE
OF OUR YOUTH AND LIFE IS FLEETING AND HAVE YOU EVER
NOTICED WHEN YOU READ STUFF IN CAPSLOCK YOU FEEL A
BIT ON EDGE HAVE YOU HAVE YOU HAVE YOU HAVE YOU
EVEN NOTICED THERE HASN'T BEEN A FULLSTOP YET I NEED
A LIE DOWN.

BUT HOW CAN YOU RELAX WHEN EVERYTHING IS SO
COMPLICATED? HAVE YOU THOUGHT AT LENGTH ABOUT WHY
BEES ARE DYING. DO YOU LIE AWAKE AT NIGHT SCREAMING
BECAUSE KITKATS ARE SLIGHTLY SMALLER NOW?

BUT SERIOUSLY, HOW CAN YOU RELAX WHEN AT LEAST TEN
PEOPLE DIE EVERY YEAR TRYING TO RELAX? DO YOU EVER SIT
STARING INTO THE ABYSS AND WONDER IF DUCKS TALK TO
EACH OTHER IN QUACKS? WHY DO BLIND PEOPLE WALK THEIR
DOGS SO MUCH? ARE COWS JUST HORSES THAT JUST MADE
POOR LIFE CHOICES?

DO YOU EVER WRITE IN CAPSLOCK TO HIDE THE FACT
THAT YOU HAVE SEVERE INSECURITY AND FIND IT EASIER
TO COMMUNICATE WITH PEOPLE IF THEY CAN'T SEE YOUR
EMOTIONS? OH, GOD!

I HOPE YOU FEEL RELAXED BECAUSE I DON'T. I felt relaxed once.
I was drinking, on a beach in the Seychelles. It was my honeymoon.
And do you know how I was repaid for my relaxation? CRABS. CRABS
EVERYWHERE! THEY CAN SMELL YOUR CALM. THEY CAN SENSE
YOUR ZEN. There is always something out there to unsettle you.
Global warming. Earthquakes. Piers Morgan.

Relaxation Tip 37:
Learn how to give your partner massages

1. Whisper in their ears

2. Start moving your hands about the place

3. Pinch their back fat

4. Bored now

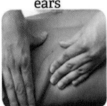   

5. This was a shit idea, wasn't it?

6. This has been going on FOREVER

7. Holy fuck, how have only five mins passed?

8. I don't know what I am doing anymore

9. Good lord, their feet are gross

10. What part of a human is this?

11. I have given up

12. What?

RIGHTS

Basic human allowances.
Like water, love and debt.

Some people don't think other people are as good as them. That is a fact. Some people live in a cloud of denial, their superiority floating slightly below their ego, believing that a person, another human being, made from the same chemicals and constructs, is below them. Seriously.

All men were created equal, according to Thomas Jefferson. In his defence, women weren't invented until some time after the signing of the US constitution. 'It's one small step for man,' whispered Neil Armstrong as he fell off an expensive space dinghy into a sandpit. In this new age of equal rights it is important not to be sexist because sexism is wrong, and being wrong is for women.

Does someone who does the exact same job as you deserve less money per month due to the organic catastrophe between their legs? Do some people not deserve to marry because they don't make love like white middle-class people (with the lights off, sometimes while listening to Enya). It's completely ridiculous. Everyone deserves to be treated fairly, to be given equal opportunity and to love.

'Gay marriage destroys the sanctity of marriage,' screams a woman who is on her third marriage.
'It's political correctness gone mad!' shouts the white man who hasn't ever left the village.
'I'm not racist BUT...' said the ignorant fucking racist person.

Every single person on this planet deserves respect. Disregard race, religion, sexuality and creed, the only thing that matters is if they listen to Mumford & Sons, and if they do, chase them out of town.

Government
Equalities Office

5th Nov 2015

Subject: New motions

Mr Cameron,
Our country is in a state of decline, and thus our department has devised new restrictions to keep the population in line.
For example:

Women should not be allowed to fly on planes. It is dangerous and their free-thinking minds could distract pilots from landing safely.

Gays should not be allowed to swim. For reasons that are made clear
in the attached 400-page document entitled 'Sharks and the homosexual'.

Differently-abled people are now to be kept solely in the North.

Immigrants now have to work 29 hours a day and earn over £200K
a week to be entitled to live in the UK.

Lesbians aren't allowed near naked flames anymore due to the likelihood that they will fire for no reason.

Black people can no longer go into motorway service stations outside the M25 for fear of people in the countryside becoming confused.

Thank you, Mr Cameron. I appreciate your time.

Maria

SELF-DEFENCE

Using someone's strength against them,
or crawling into a ball and weeping,
whichever works for you.

How would you defend yourself against a house fire? The tip here is to set yourself on fire a little bit every day until you become immune to fire. How do you survive getting stabbed? Get vaccinated against stabbings. What happens if you start drowning? Learn to speak dolphin to ensure rescue. It's easy, you just need to be prepared.

If we have learnt anything from Liam Neeson movies post-2005, it's that the only way to protect your family is to be able to kick people really hard in the face. The world is a dangerous place. People out there are wanting to mug you and your family and even your dog. Wasps exist. Katie Hopkins could be in your fridge right now, waiting, lurking. Can you defend your family? Can you protect them? The only way to ensure the safety of those you love is to have your house in a permanent state of *Home Alone*-style readiness. Advise those you care about where the traps are. And just wait.

If you are worried about these sorts of dangers there are a few solutions you can explore. First, never leave your house. One hundred per cent of outdoor accidents happen outdoors. Outside your house lies a world of swords, horses and horses made of swords. You don't need this. Make sure you have plenty of drinking water in your house; if you can't get drinking water, sipping vodka will do. The human body can survive for 12 weeks on nothing but Wotsits. Wotsits are the only food that can't be destroyed by a nuclear blast. You may be dead, but your food supply will live on forever.

How to survive various animal attacks

Bears:
Roll into a ball and start rolling towards it threateningly.

Sharks:
Boop it on the nose. If that doesn't work, boop it in the dick

Wolves:
Throw a stick or something. Or tell it to sit. Never seen a wolf actually.

Geese:
Your time has come. There is no way out.

Wasps:
Apparently this wasp is the size of a goose so you're fucked.

Snake:
According to Disney's Robin Hood, turn it into a balloon.

Spiders:
Just set everything on fire. Everything. Even you.

Crocodiles:
Fill it with clocks. Captain Hook does that and survives for a bit.

Cats:
Can be punted up to 20m in extreme situations.

Not that my first thought about most situations is to set your house on fire, but this is the correct way to deal with spiders:

CAREFULLY TRY TO
CAPTURE SPIDER IN
A GLASS

THROW GLASS
AT DEMON
CREATURE

USE A HOOVER
TO HUMANELY
REMOVE SPIDER

HOOVER IS FULL OF
PREVIOUSLY
IMPRISONED SPIDERS.
PANIC

USE FLY SPRAY AS
A LAST MEASURE

RATIONALLY
SET FIRE TO
THE SPRAY

REALISE YOU ARE
A USELESS HUMAN

MOVE HOUSE

Sleep

Human buffering.

Bedtime is that special time of the night, where you stop looking at Twitter on the sofa, and go and lie in the dark and look at Twitter. It's also a time where you lie in a state of perpetual agony going over every embarrassing thing you have ever done. Your body has been screaming at you all day, shouting about how tired you are, begging for coffee and failing at being productive. You finally settle under your duvet, and your brain says, 'Oh hi, yeah, we've been pretty tired all day, but doesn't this seem like the ideal opportunity to think about that time when you were 20 and got beat up by a bunch of kids?' Maybe that's just me.

Insomnia is the enemy of sleep. It's the tiny part of your brain that can't switch off. The body is wanting sleep, it's craving rest, but the brain just can't stop working. Insomnia breaks you down, leaves you useless during the day and meaningless at night. I tried valerian root, sleeping pills and that weird lavender spray that makes your pillow smell like a 2am screening of *Calendar Girls*. NOTHING. The worst part about insomnia is that it's just really boring. You don't buy an old abandoned house in a bad area, you don't start a fight club, and you don't get a sweet double personality that gets to be rude with Helena Bonham Carter. I mostly lie thinking about work, and when I have done that for a bit I contemplate the meaning of life and what I am doing on this planet but then Sky News starts talking about sex toys or Babestation start discussing the rise of Islamic militarisation in the Middle East and nothing ever makes sense again.

Facts about sleep

Sleeping for
eight hours
a night is unnatural
how do you do it
please teach me.

Not getting
enough sleep
has been linked
to erectile
dysfunction
and guns.

The most common
reasons for
sleeping disorders
are:

Stress

That time in Year 5
when Nick said
I had massive tits.

Worrying

Spiders

Gravy regret

Netflix

While there is no conclusive
evidence that there are
monsters under the bed,
Sleeping with a machete is
recommended.

The average
human
person eats
600
people in
their sleep
in their
lifetime.

You are 12 times
more likely to be
eaten by a bear
in your sleep.

The average sleeping pill
contains hair, Bourbon,
an Edith Piaf record and
sloth wee.

SOCIAL MEDIA

A way of arguing with strangers that doesn't get you banned from the pub.

What kind of person do you want to be? When you were ten did you dream of becoming a vet? A fireman? A superhero? A 30-year-old slightly overweight weirdo covered in crisps on a Saturday night? Did the ten-year-old you think you would be taking pictures of your dinner and sharing them for the admiration of strangers? Did they think you would be sending pictures of your genitals to prospective mates by contorting yourself while holding a phone?

This age is one of capture. Of saving a moment you feel precious to you. If it's a simple pleasure such as a meal then you can Instagram it. If it's a pleasant day with people you don't hate, then you can Facebook it. If it's a crap joke or an observation on a horrible celebrity, then you can tweet it. Or if it's just that you're a bit bored and want a strange hairy man with massive hands to disappoint you for 20 minutes, you can Tinder it.

As UK law now attempts to regulate social media, it's worth remembering some of the headlines that have shaped internet law.

At the end of the day, the internet is a bar. It's a bar with many rooms, playing any sort of music you like, with crowds of people from all walks of life – it's just up to you which table you choose to sit at.

	Pintrest	Twitter	Facebook
Mostly used by	White women who really really like curtains	People who must thrust their opinions at other people	New mothers and racist people
Mostly used for	Looking at Kitchens, Dogs, Nail art and trumpets I don't know	Screaming at strangers and telling celebrities to shit off	Posting pictures of racist babies
Best for people that	Have no money but are pretty sure that one day they will have all the money	Don't really have a lot on, but still need to feel fairly self-important	Like sharing pictures that let all of your friends know that you're now a racist
Not suitable if you	Hate things from IKEA that have been made to look like things from a skip	Don't want to hear other people's opinions, or can't back up your arguments	Are not racist

Instagram	Google +	LinkedIn
Teenagers and sex offenders	Very very lonely people	Coke addled bankers and people who don't go out much
Taking pictures of your own face and deleting them when they get 0 likes	No one is entirely sure	Stalking receptionists
Really really really really really really like their own face	I have no idea about this one either	Think they are fucking awesome even though they work in accounts
Are not attractive and only take pictures of benches or plants or something	Enjoy decent social media platforms.	Are actually busy at work and don't have time for this shit

SPORT

Critiquing athletes on their physical prowess while getting pissed.

The greatest sport ever invented is Bo-Taoshi. This is a fact. Bo-Taoshi is a game where people run at each other, use each other as a climbing frame and try to get to the top of a very large pole. That's it. The second greatest sport ever invented is inverted binocular football. It is exactly how it sounds. Sport should be ridiculous. Since when was football more of a sport than Quidditch? When did rugby become better than dog surfing?

The basic premise of 90% of sports is GET THAT THING OVER THERE. But the rules are what make them different. For example, the offside rule in football:

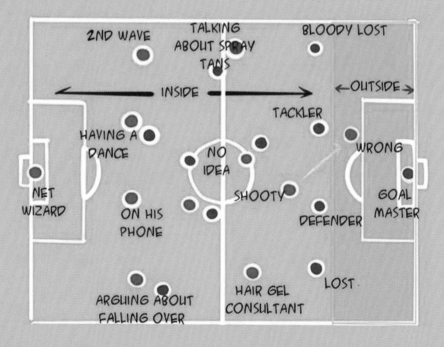

Also, have you ever tried to explain golf to someone? It's almost impossible.

Anything can be a sport if you put money on it. Yet sport is a billion-dollar business, kicking a sphere into a mesh can now earn you more than a small country's GDP. The role models for young men now are ladish idiots with false egos and fat wallets. The corruption is everywhere, from Bernie Ecclestone throwing money at anyone with the surname 'Judge' just in case, to Sepp Blatter shaking hands with more undesirables than Satan at a 'Complete Bastards' meeting. Can it still be fun with all this bullshit flying around it? All sports should include a round where puppies play for both sides for ten minutes.

I'm going to watch some more Bo-Taoshi.

A Guide To Sports

Football
"Get the ball.... over there"

Tennis
"Get the ball.... over there"

Rugby
"Get the ball.... over there"

Cricket
"Get the ball.... over there...in the next six days"

Formula 1
"Go in circles please"

Golf
"Get the ball.... over there, but with 100% more trousers"

Boxing
"Twat that other human"

Table Tennis
"This is stupid"

Bowling
"Skittles for people that hate outside"

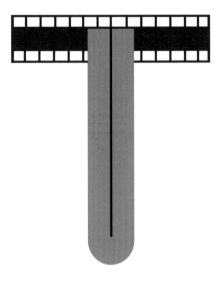

TALKING

Throwing vowels out of your mouth
at other people.

Is the art of conversation dying? Are we becoming a species that would rather text than talk? Yes. Conversations are horrible. For someone with anxiety a conversation with someone you don't know is essentially *The Krypton Factor* for antisocial weirdos.

The British aren't very good at excusing themselves from a conversation. We say things like 'Well, I will let you get on', which means 'This amount of human interaction is causing me physical pain, I must leave and lie down' or 'I won't keep you', which means 'I wasn't keeping you anyway, but I need to run as far away from this as humanly possible'. Talking with Brits is the equivalent of that annoying little dance you do with people on pavements: when they start going one way, you go the same way, you smile, then do the same thing the other way, then want to stab them to death for getting in the bloody way.

The real reason I attempt to avoid human interaction as much as possible is one conversation that has always haunted me. Upon ordering a coffee, the young barista handed me my latte and said, 'Enjoy your coffee' to which I, in full British mode, replied, 'Thanks, you too!'. I have lain awake playing this awful situation over in my head so many times. If I were to be able to travel in time, killing Hitler would be a close second to altering my retort upon this travesty of a social interaction.

THERAPY

Using words to sort out your head box.

'How was the relationship with your father?' 'Do you think you start fires as a way to deal with your break up with Sophie when you were nine?' 'Why are you throwing pencils at me?' There are many types of therapy. The one where another human being sits there asking you questions, the type where you find relaxation and mindfulness through fitness and exercise, or the one where you drink until you can't feel feelings anymore. I find the latter to be the most effective.

More and more people are in therapy nowadays, mostly because more and more people are feeling a tad squiffy in their mind tank due to a pressurised society devoted to promoting excellence. Mediocrity is a damn fine quality: you don't need to excel, you can just be you, even if you are a little bit brainbonked.

I have avoided therapy, mostly due to cowardice. I fear that the person sat opposite me would provoke some deep, dark, repressed memory resulting in Vietnam-style flashbacks about a schoolboy trauma. I lie. I went to therapy once, and I would like to emphasise that this is true, my therapist told me I was using alcohol as an escape mechanism, then took me for a pint in the pub next door after the session. This may be when I lost faith in the practice.

Personally, I use Twitter as therapy. I talk to 40x40 pixel avatars going through similar situations to me. Their anonymity and selfless honesty provides a much-needed respite from my own brain. So many people on this forum of bedlam are willing to help strangers, to talk you down or pick you up, for no other reason than to help. I can imagine this is a terribly unhealthy way to feel normal. But if it works, it works; some people run, some people lie on the sofa, I talk. It's reassuring to know that whatever state you are in, whatever situation has befallen you, that you are not alone, and there will always be someone out there willing to help you.

TRAVEL

Going to the other side of the world to use the internet.

If I had money, and didn't need to work to afford a house, or food, or a wife, I would be a traveller. I would wander the continents in a pair of badly-fitting flip-flops, condescendingly dispensing advice to other travellers in local bars, telling them about things other tourists never get to see. I would eat horrible food and pretend I liked it, I would grow my hair long and never wash it, then complain about no one finding me attractive. I would take selfies next to ancient statues, post them online and discuss over the internet how much fun I am having while I don't leave the Wi-Fi hotspot for fear of being left alone with my thoughts.

Travelling is different to a holiday. It is an excuse to get lost, to go solo, to emphasise your independence while spending your parents' money. You don't stay in hotels, you stay in hostels – creepy rooms above bars with 16 beds per room and a stain on the floor that definitely came out of someone. You offend local cultures by dressing like them, eating like them, and longing for a meal of sausage and chips as another raw octopus testicle is put in front of you.

In any language the things you need to know that are essential to your wanderings, are:

'Hello'
'Thank you'
'Two beers, please'
'Where the bloody fuck am I?'
'Coffee. Now. Thanks'
'I'm just a girl, standing in front of a sexy foreign bartender, asking him to help me disappoint my parents'

~T

THE DIFFERENT PEOPLE YOU MEET WHILE TRAVELLING:

The Australian backpacker
who knows more than you

The Gap Yeah girl getting
life experience

The bitter ex-pat who loves
Britain but won't live there

The pissed-up, loud
American

TROLL

Someone who disagrees with you online.

Once upon a time trolls lived under bridges and posed riddles at you to let you get past. Today, trolls are usually bored people with awful body odours, who scour the internet to locate vulnerable people to torture. This is mostly down to a severe lack of self-worth and misplaced hatred but they are a very prominent part of millennial life. People have been given jail time for trolling people on the internet. The days of sitting at your computer and pretending to be a 13-year-old girl to fool creepy old men are over: we are all being watched, your internet history shall be written on your tombstone.

A troll's attacks can vary from a 'Oh God, you're shit at this, aren't you?' to heinous threats involving things I would rather not say. They get off on the fact that they annoy you. They validate their own existence by making yours slightly worse. The best example of this is *The Sun* columnist Katie Hopkins, who is the human equivalent of getting your scrotum trapped in your flies. It's an endless cycle: they write something abhorrent, it goes viral because it is so disgusting, it is read to be critiqued and, due to such high traffic, the company would be foolish not to employ this person again.

It's hard to ignore this ignorance. You want to grab them by the shoulders and scream how wrong they are in their faces, but you know that all you will get in return is a smug grin and a retort of how you are attacking their values. As long as everyone is allowed to have an opinion, people will continue to have the wrong ones and THIS IS WHY FREE SPEECH CAN'T WORK. Oh God, I'm turning into a Tory! I need a lie down.

If you want to know what a troll is like in real life, here is walking bollock Katie Hopkins' day planner:

09.00am – Tell children Santa Claus doesn't exist

09.30am – Punch a cat in the face

10.00am – Go on the morning TV, tell someone to shit off

10.30am – Kick a homeless man

11.00am – Hail the Dark Lord

11.30am – Go on Twitter, write something controversial

12.00pm – Tell cup of tea to fuck off

12.30pm – Bang a stranger in a field

13.00pm – Yell racial slurs at swans

13.30pm – Phone kids at school, tell them I hate them

14.00pm – Twitter again

14.30pm – Punt a hedgehog over a fence

15.00pm – Sacrifice a goat

15.30pm – Pick up kids from school, run over a dog on the way home

16.00pm – Drink wine

UKIP

Members of Slytherin House who got kicked out for being a bit too radical.

If one political party was to be the subject of a situational comedy, UKIP would be that party. Their members have famously said that storms were the fault of gay marriage, that the traffic on the M1 is the fault of Romanian immigrants and that women just need 'a shag' and to 'Shut up'. So they really are a party with their finger on the pulse.

UKIP's infamous leader, Nigel Farage, a cross between Kim Jong-un and a suit filled with plasticine, is a man with a vendetta. He hates Europe so much he married a German, who he employs with taxpayer money as his secretary. He has said over and over again that he is not a racist, while he has been heard to use the N-word in casual conversation. He does come across as charming, and as one of the people, but in fact he doesn't give a shit about the people. The people are those working in the shops, the delivery drivers and the petrol station workers. The nurses and bus drivers. Nigel Farage is not a man of the people, he is a man unto himself, a man whose favourite answer is 'Um well, yes, yes, well, yes' and his default retort is 'WELL, EUROPE' For example:

'NIGEL, WHAT WOULD YOU LIKE FOR DINNER?'
'WELL, THE THING ABOUT EUROPE IS...'
'NO, NIGEL, TEA, FOOD... WHAT DO YOU WANT?'
'TO RID THE BARNETT FORMULA'
'FOR THE SAKE OF FUCK, NIGEL, WHAT SHOULD I COOK?'
'THOSE FUCKING BULGARIANS!'

If you think UKIP are alright, raise your arm. Your right arm. At a 70-degree angle from your body. Point out all your fingers. There you go.

[Inaudible racist bollocks]

Scaremongering fucktrumpet convinces middle class white people to blame everything they did on other people

🕐 14 May 2015 | UK Politics

Nigel Farage, looking like a ballbag stretched over a mannequin

A quite well-off white man has used words to make sure the generation responsible for the current state of Britain believe that all our county's problems can blamed on foreign people, because that's just loads easier.

Nigel Forage, with his face that people would pay money to hit, used his racism to brainwash morons.

Just look at his stupid bloody face the prick.

UBER

Taxis for people who
work in media.

The main problem with Uber drivers is that they pick you up in their own transportation, and no one, NO ONE, turns up with a horse. Your job is to transport your customers to their destination in a cheap and easy manner, yet you never get an uber driver with a segway and a sidecar, a skateboard and a pull-along wagon, or a ferret-powered go-kart. Living in this mundane world, getting a man who smells of beef picking you up in a Prius, is hardly revolutionary.

Ubers are cheaper than black cabs, and as fares are predetermined, this usually means a journey from Waterloo to Shoreditch won't go via Bristol. Yet, as they are driven by people who just have nothing better to do, you can get a driver who is really rather pleasant, or one who, like I got a few weeks ago, believes that Jesus is coming back some time in September 2016 and is 'going to shit everyone up'.

Uber are a very caring company, though. In December of 2014 during the Sydney siege, where three people died, they raised their fares by 400% due to people wanting to leave the affected area. Whenever you hear a cabbie moan about Ubers, you can hear the CEO rubbing his hands together like a Bond villain before launching into a pool of money.

There are certain advantages to taxis over public transport. The scent of bodily odour is more like a sausage trapped in a toaster than a bear exploding in a kebab fire. You won't feel another human being's genitals against your back unless you tip too much, and if there's a strange Irishman singing folk songs next to you then you've probably just got in the wrong car.

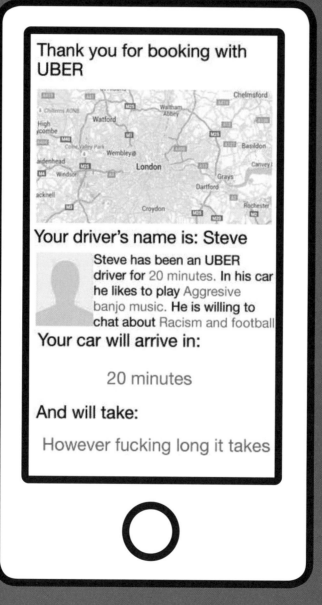

Thank you for booking with UBER

Your driver's name is: Steve

Steve has been an UBER driver for 20 minutes. In his car he likes to play Aggressive banjo music. He is willing to chat about Racism and football

Your car will arrive in:

20 minutes

And will take:

However fucking long it takes

UNHAPPINESS

And other negative states of mind.

As a depressive you tend to view the world negatively. You see the worst in everything, mostly because your brain is wired to prepare yourself for disappointment. I blame most of this not on the state of my mental health, but in fact on being a Scottish Rugby supporter. You learn, after years of supporting Scotland in their never-ending bid to come last in every competition, not to get your hopes up. If they finish the game with a few points it is much better than finishing with none. Yes, they may not have won, or succeeded in their falsely planned triumphs, but they were there, they tried and one day, maybe, there will be a positive result.

Being a pessimist isn't about finding everything in the world appalling, it's about not getting your hopes up. Scotland may never win the Six Nations, but my God, they will turn up, work their arses off and even if they do fail, they tried. This is the least any of us can do. Graveyards are littered with people who didn't try, who couldn't be bothered to turn up.

Some things, however, are easy to see the negative in. The general public are a quivering mass of complete gits; television is filled with people who need to get in the bin. It's a fine line between pessimism and realism, but not expecting much is not a crime. Kids today are given prizes for just turning up, then wonder why their nine-to-five jobs aren't rewarding them on a daily basis for just being on time.

The gritty reality is that most things won't pay off. Luck is reserved for the idiots, success is reserved for those who failed MULTIPLE TIMES.

You fuck up, you move on. You make a mistake, you accept it and never make that mistake again. For those interested, this chapter is available as a motivational poster you can share on Facebook with your friends who aren't doing that well at the moment.

Optimist

"This glass is half-full"

Pessimist

"This glass is half-empty"

Realist

"I didn't want a glass of water I wanted rum"

Surrealist

"What kind of dog is this?"

Really angry, stubborn Canadians.

America is the kid who ran away from home at 12, found a new place to live, then had a little bit of a mental breakdown that no one has ever really addressed at family dinners since. To a Brit, America looks like this:

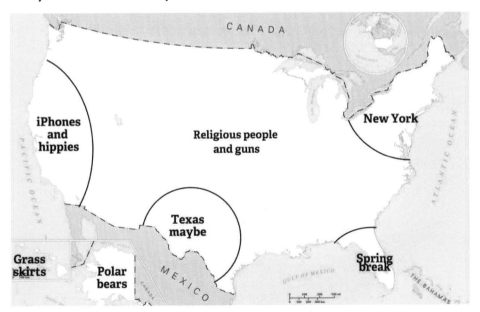

The annoying thing is, and it REALLY is annoying, is that Americans have done quite well for themselves. Yeah, they don't have our charm, our patience or our grace, but they have a TV channel dedicated PURELY to Spanish soap operas. It is a well-known fact that every

American is 20% guns, 20% ego, 20% Twinkie, 20% Bruce Springsteen and 30% bad at maths. (Also, if you're American and you're reading this, there is an S on the end of the word maths. You've misplaced that S on the end of Lego for some bloody stupid reason.)

Ignoring the obvious and relentless issues with America, we have to focus on the positives. This is the country that gave us Twizzlers, *Star Wars*, Anna Kendrick, *Parks and Recreation*, Twitter and Jazz. So it's not all bad. Yeah, the police force are more racist than a drunken Mel Gibson in a synagogue, and their government are more concerned with flying metal death birds over third-world countries and blowing up schools than addressing a woman's right to her own body, but have you seen the *Fast and Furious* films? THEY. ARE. FUCKING. AWESOME.

And soon we shall get to witness the Presidential election. POLITICS ON SPEED DIRECTED BY MICHAEL BAY. Billions are spent on deciding the next RULER OF EARTH. Will it be the right-wing person? Or the slightly less right-wing person?

Americans are egomaniacs because they make things like the world series then don't let other countries compete and declare themselves world champions.

TIP: You can pretend to be an American in the UK by smacking the front of taxi cabs and shouting, 'HAY I'M WALKEN HARE' before going to a Republican rally or something. I don't know, I am very tired. Is it the end of the book yet? Fuck, I just looked, there's ages to go. Dammit!

~U

American To English
Translation Guide

Chips	Crisps
Fries	Chips
House	Cottage
Sidewalk	Pavement
Trash Can	Rubbish box
Gun	Shooty bang
Route	Direction
Cookie	Crunch circle
Football	Kick goal
Gas	Windy pops
Toilet	Noisy throne
Freeway	Traffic lane
Cops	Bobbies
Diapers	Nasty sacks
Sneakers	Jolly bottoms

VALIDATION

Feeling like a special snowflake in a crowd of other special snowflakes.

We all want to feel validated in our lives. Be it from our parents, our peers or strangers on the internet. We all just want to feel like we are using this limited time on this planet to justify our existence. There is no harm in wanting to feel this way, and striving to make others happy, proud or feel better. The harm in validation comes from false praise. I mean, you get a prom for finishing pre-school now. You get an award FOR FINGER PAINTING or not gouging your eyes out or whatever you do at pre-school. False praise is what causes headlines that finish with the words,' And then they turned the gun on themselves'.

Every single person online wants to be validated. They want someone to like their selfie, they want someone to favourite their joke, because it's nice to know that someone, anyone, gives a shit about their mundane life. We can't all be rockstars and sex symbols but, hell, I will do my UTMOST to try and make a couple of people laugh a day, and if you have something interesting, a valid opinion or an original viewpoint to share, why shouldn't you? Even if it isn't to everyone's taste, at least you tried.

However, internet validation is false validation. Being popular on Twitter is like being a millionaire in Zimbabwe: meaningless. Getting addicted to likes, shares and retweets can become very real, though, and can become the only outlet for some young people to feel like their lives are worth anything. It's important not to get caught up in this forum of self-validation as then you end up as a hunchbacked CREEP typing weird nonsense into a book that only weird people will read. OH GOD, I HAVE SAID TOO MUCH!

A NOTE FROM THE AUTHOR:

I am hideously aware of the irony embedded in this chapter. Three hundred words about validation and here I am, screaming at you for God knows how many pages for your approval. Let's be honest, we are getting near the end of the book here. I am tired, you are tired, we are all tired. We all need a holiday. Somewhere nice where the cocktails taste like ambrosia and the bartenders look like the people you see in magazines. But here we are. And I apologise. I am very tired. I haven't slept in years. Everything sounds like corners. My thoughts are now entirely in capslock.

I doubt the publishers will have checked this far into the book so I think we can get away with this.

So if you could just imagine a really funny picture that would have the potential to go viral, that would be brilliant. I would really appreciate it. I won't tell if you don't. Look, if you see me about, I will buy you a drink by way of an apology.

I appreciate your discretion.

VEGETARIANISM

People trying to be rabbits.

First of all, there is nothing wrong with being a vegetarian. OK.
Secondly, this is everything that is wrong with being a vegetarian.

1. We grew incisors so we could attack defenceless animals with our mouths.
2. If pigs didn't want to be eaten, they wouldn't taste like bacon.
3. If I could eat a unicorn, I would eat a unicorn.
4. We don't eat dogs because they are fucking awesome.
5. We don't eat cats because they probably taste like shit.
6. Yes animal cruelty is bad.
7. If fruit tasted like steak, everything would be fine.

Certain animals need to be eaten. It's how they evolved. If a cow doesn't get milked, it fills up and up and up and eventually explodes in a creamy mess. So we have to milk it, and then turn it into steaks because that's what the cow would have wanted. If we don't carve up pigs, they can become sentient and take hostages. If we don't eat chickens, they will just keep laying eggs until every flat surface is eggs, everything is eggs, your children drown in eggs. Do you want your children to drown? Thought not. Kill the chickens.

'How do you know you've got a vegetarian at a dinner party? They're the one ruining the atmosphere talking about how your dinner was waterboarded'. Vegetarians and vegans are fine, but a certain amount of ego goes hand in hand with this diet. Militant vegetarians like members of PETA are the best example of this: they are quite brilliant at getting their message completely wrong. 'THOUSANDS OF CHICKENS DIED TO MAKE SURE YOU CAN EAT EGGS' or 'HORSES ARE MEANT FOR GOING INTO BATTLE, NOT LASAGNES' pfft.

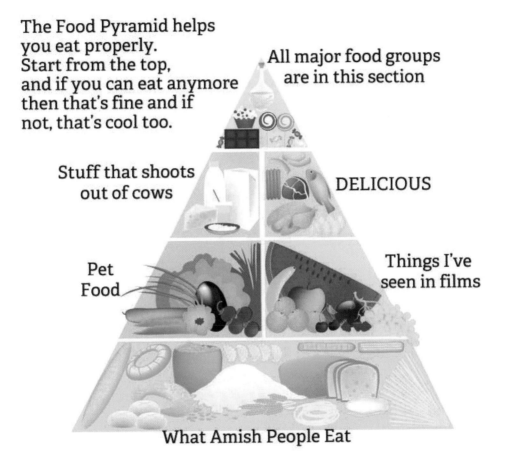

The Food Pyramid helps you eat properly. Start from the top, and if you can eat anymore then that's fine and if not, that's cool too.

All major food groups are in this section

Stuff that shoots out of cows

DELICIOUS

Pet Food

Things I've seen in films

What Amish People Eat

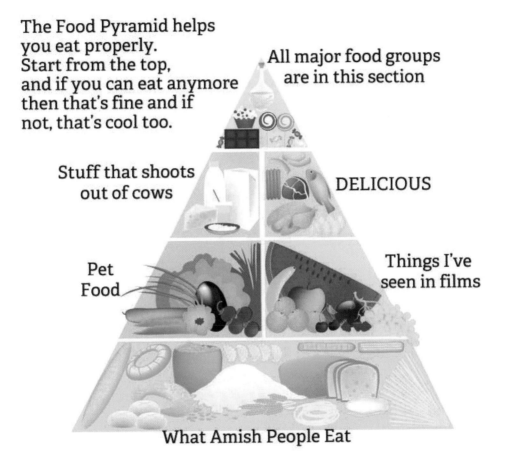

~V

VIDEO GAMES

Like Monopoly but on a TV and with punching.

Video games have a horrific effect on our youth. In 1996 a young man from Florida folded his entire family at 90-degree angles after playing Tetris. In 2004 a woman from Pennsylvania ate 6,000 cherries in one day and told the police it was because she was being chased by ghosts after playing Pac-Man. In 2007, a man from Birmingham was jailed for stealing ladders from people's swimming pools after playing *The Sims*. The video game series *Grand Theft Auto* has been responsible for many young men thinking you can get into a strip club while wearing tracksuit bottoms.

It's difficult to draw a line between reality and video games nowadays. I find myself thinking I am in a game while talking to other people, often spinning in circles and running into walls whilst they are talking to me, as if they were a non-playable character. There are telltale ways to bring yourself back to reality though. For instance, turtles don't make other cars spin around when you throw them out of your car in real life. Most archaeologists aren't pixelated women with triangular breasts, and taking mushrooms doesn't make you twice as big, usually the opposite.

The biggest danger to our youth in regard to video games is the lies they now tell. I was playing against a young man on *Call of Duty* a few weeks ago, and he told me that he had fornicated with my mother. I rang my mother, and luckily she had never heard of NoobMaster05. So now I must spend the rest of my days clearing my mother's name. I will find you, NoobMaster05, and I will fold your family into 90-degree angles.

HOW TO WRITE A VIDEO GAME
Pick a character for the lead. Your choices are:
A burly, middle-aged white dude
That's it. That's your option.

Now, what is he fighting?
Zombies
Aliens
Zombie Aliens
An oppressive regime that your character doesn't agree with.

Now, why is he fighting them?
THEY KILLED HIS DAUGHTER
THEY KILLED HIS WIFE
THEY KILLED HIS DOG.

What personal attributes does your character have?
Angry
Angry
Really Angry
Angry with a drinking problem.

What can he do?
Martial arts for no reason
Use loads of guns for no reason
Punch people in the tits until their eyes fly out.

You have your basis. Now just create a bunch of levels where bad guys show up for no reason and beat them up until your character feels better about himself. I'll take 5% of your profit.

V😦MITING

Exorcisms for alcohol.

Everyone has a good spewing story. You can be sat with people you have only known for ten minutes, and you can be roaring with laughter at a good tale of projectile embarrassment. While I should not be encouraging young people to binge drink, hence resulting in a gob explosion, it is something everyone needs to go through at one stage in their life.

An evening of drinking and then reversing your wallet out of your mouth into a toilet is an important stage of learning who you really are. Until you have spent a night with your head on the toilet seat, feeling sorry for yourself and wondering where it all went wrong, you will never understand who you really are. However, I can tell you: you are a mess. We are all gigantic messes walking around pretending to be upstanding members of society.

That person who just served you a sandwich in Pret? At some point in their life they drank too much Irn-Bru and vodka and did a hoop into their parents' pot plant. The person who made you your Michelin star rabbit leg that cost you 300 quid at some point whitied on the front of a Ford Fiesta and blew sludge all over a hedge. We are all the same. Every single person in this entire world, be they rich or poor, upper or lower class, famous or unknown, is at the exact same level in life when they are gushing out of their faces. It is one of the only times all human beings are truly awful. That, and cum faces, but I didn't want to write a chapter on that.

Why do you vomit?

Step 6: Chunder Everywhaa

Step 1.
You put something down your gob that your body didn't agree to have put into it. Much like your ex-partner.

Step 5.
What only went down moments ago returns to your teeth case, but now it's angry and wants to be freed. And freed all over the wall of a pub bathroom it shall be.

Step 2.
Look at the fucking state of this. This is a beautiful mass of flesh and guts. It evolved to process materials, not suffer 3am shots of Sambuca.

Step 4.
After the stomach has booted it out there is no choice left. It is inevitable. There is no turning back. There is no help for you. There is no God.

Step 3. Once the gunk meets your stomach, the stomach takes one look at it and goes "Nah mate" like a bouncer at a Soho club.

WANKING

Making yourself feel better without having to bother someone else.

If you are of a sensitive disposition, or easily offended please look away now. Right, have they gone? Phew, what shall we talk about? FISTING? No. OK, let's just carry on.

I, for one, don't masturbate. It is a sin. God is everywhere, and I certainly don't want Her watching me as I disgrace myself. If you masturbate too much, you go blind, but if you go blind then you get a free guide dog, so maybe self-pleasure is simply the path to free dogs. What the fuck am I on about? Let's try this again.

Everybody masturbates. People who say they don't are LIARS and probably do something much much worse. (Refer to the word in the first paragraph in capital letters, but by themselves.)

Wanking is no longer an activity done alone in the confines of your bedroom, the laptop screen shining on your face resulting in a moment of disgust and instant regret as soon as you have completed your objective. It now affects every aspect of our lives. Social masturbation is the act of making yourself feel important to impress others. Unlike hand-to-gland combat, it won't get you kicked out of your office. Instead of throwing your genitals around like a man trying to control a garden hose in a tornado, you simply stroke your own ego.

We've all been sat talking to people whose favourite conversation is themselves. A quick tip for anyone who does that: instead of boring people with your own self-importance, simply run in front of a mirror and look at your stupid gurning face. Horrible, isn't it? No one else wants to see this. Stop it.

Arguing with bombs.

War is like a game of chess: the important people sit at the back, the pawns go in and do everything, then it all goes terribly wrong and suddenly the chess board is on fire and the rook is explaining on ITV how this was unavoidable.

There have been many important wars in history that have been forgotten. (All of these are true.) The Great Emu War of 1932, where the Australian Army went to war with... Emus. (The Australian Army lost.) In 1788 the Austrian Army split into two factions to attack the Turks. After getting a bit discombobulated, they attacked themselves. In 2004, giant Russian crabs (yes, crabs), thought to be a military experiment, accidentally attacked Norway. Basically, war is idiotic and unnecessary, unless you have gigantic militarised crabs on your side.

There is only one solution to gain a perfect harmony amongst all races, all religions and all peoples of this bizarrely divided world.

Eurovision. The single greatest annual event ever invented. Nations and peoples come together to celebrate camp dance music and forced ballads in an expression of love and acceptance. And Russia are in it. If every country in the world was to star in a Eurovision-style competition, world peace would happen within days. 'Yes, you may have nukes, but your third key change was fantastic so we forgive you'. The blood in the streets would be replaced with glitter. Wind machines would replace war machines. The planet would come together, and as a united world, would still give Britain nil points.

~W

We asked some British people to name these guns
Here is what they thought.

WELSH

AND OTHER LANGUAGES

Because some people won't learn English.
The selfish sods!

I experimented with being bilingual in college but I found myself drawn to a single language. I can, however, ask for 'another beer' in France, Spain, America, Japan, The United Arab Emirates and Yorkshire.

For those unaccustomed to other languages, or those scared to go abroad because they DON'T SELL CHIPS or ARE NICE, here is a guide to languages.

Welsh – Like an old man spitting at you as he falls down an elevator shaft.

English – English is fucking mad! It's tough to be thorough through the thought of throwing this concept around.

French – French sounds like vowels being forced through a moustache. After defining if the apple is female or male (it's neither, it's a fucking apple!), you have to count. And it's not normal counting, it's French counting.

Spanish – Spanish sounds like the host's tongue has become sentient and decided to rebel against language.

German – The language of love, where every beautiful thought is vocalised in a way that to the ears appears to be a dog choking in Klingon.

American – Like English? But everything is a question? For no reason? Like, all the time?

Japanese – Shouting. It's all just shouting. Either angry shouting or screaming.

Arabic – The language that spells fear in the hearts of scared middle-class white people all around the world.

Scottish – Like English but on fast forward and the tape got a bit mangled so now it's kind of hard to listen to.

Australian – Also like English, but every word is spoken as if you resent the English.

Those are the important languages. All others are merely noises from other languages smacked together for little or no purpose. Remember, if in doubt, simply use your GCSE knowledge and ask for the library, on a Tuesday, is it busy? how's the bread?

Lets learn some fun foreign
Swear words!

KISAMA
(lord of the donkeys)
Japanese

RunKnisse
(You masturbating gnome)
Norwegian

Jebiesz Jeze!
(You fuck hedghogs)
Polish

Jy's 'n hondenaaier
(You're a dog fucker)
Afrikaans

Fatdu I Rassgat!
(Jump up your own arse)
Icelandic

U wot m8 I'll bosh
your noggin
(pardon me sir, I'll hit you in the head)
British

Ni Mi La Bi
(your mother catches turtles)
Mandarin

WRATH

And how if we don't sin, Jesus died for nothing.

The cardinal sins were written down by people with not a lot going on, to convince other people with not a lot going on, not to do too much. In our age of technology, we deal with the seven sins our ancestors feared so much in our day-to-day.

LUST – PORNHUB. You can now get whatever depraved, filthy fetish you want online at the click of a button. You can watch Peruvian warthog foot porn before church. You can find hot singles in your area and then get a doctor to sort out the hot tingles in your area.

ENVY – INSTAGRAM. With the swipe of a finger you can lurk in the shadow of other people's lives, staring at their fancy breakfast while you eat your mouldy toast, and salivating over their Louboutins as your five-year-old Converse fall apart.

GLUTTONY – JUST EAT. If you touch a piece of metal in your hand in the right way, you can get food delivered to your door, whenever you want. It's disgusting, it's deplorable, it's fucking brilliant! When you can finally get zoos and cigarettes delivered in the same way, we will have peaked as a species.

WRATH – TWITTER. When you get angry with a celebrity or furious about a piece of journalism, you can take to the internet, smash your raging thoughts into your keyboard and make your parents proud by telling other people to shit off. Nothing quite says 'I am a serious human being' like threatening another human being from the safety of an anonymous account.

GREED – eBAY. Need a lamp in the shape of Dean Gaffney? Need a rug with pictures of wolves attacking the Uyghur people of north-west China? Need condoms made of Lego? OF COURSE NOT. But you can buy them all anyway because you got drunk and used one-click purchasing and you are a grown-up person with the ability to make their own poor choices.

SLOTH – SIRI. You don't even need to use your thumbs anymore. You can literally shout at a rectangle to text your mum for you. However sometimes autocorrect and Siri don't mix. 'SIRI, TAKE THE WHEEL'; 'Searching for takeaways in Wales'; 'FOR THE SAKE OF FUCK, SIRI, THEY'RE SHOOTING AT US'; 'Calling Marcus.'

PRIDE – FACEBOOK. Do you know who wants to see pictures of your babies? NO ONE. EVER. YOUR BABY LOOKS LIKE EVERYONE ELSE'S BABY. Facebook allows you to constantly shove your success in your high-school friend's faces. Remember Sophie in Year 6 who wouldn't go out with you? Well, now she can read your misinformed opinions on foreign policy and how you spent too much money on a badly-decorated flat.

X FACTOR

A study of reality TV and how human beings need to be stopped.

Reality TV, where 'normal' and 'everyday' people can become famous. I emphasise the words 'normal' and 'everyday' because the people on these shows are anything but. They all have a sob story, they all have some form of undiagnosed mental condition, and are so shameless in their attempts to become famous that they would give a rabid bear a handjob for a 20-second segment on a TV show. The worst part is the sob stories. The 'pity me, I am a real person with real problems, but my problems are more important because I am on the television' stories that get trotted out like a prize-winning pig in every TV contest.

To make your own *The Only Way Is Essex* action figure, all you need to do is vacuum pack a sack of oranges. You can play *The Voice* at home by turning your chair away from your family when you don't like what is coming out of their mouths. You can pretend to be Simon Cowell by letching unashamedly at dogs on the street.

So, *The X Factor*, a competition that takes 700 weeks to find the ONE PERSON who can release the worst Christmas single ever forced into your eardrums. The presenters are people you've never heard of, who all look like water-damaged Playmobil people. A person chucks some vowels out of themselves and the audience goes crazy. It's the Roman amphitheatre of our time, but instead of lions being released when you're shit, you get tabloid reporters going through your bins.

ON X FACTOR YOU GET SIX TYPES OF CONTESTANT:

The attractive 30-year-old bloke mums can fancy

The mother whose sob story is that she had kids and kids ruined her freedom and she needs three months away from her kids

The arrogant hipster who thinks he is brilliant but doesn't care but does care

The woman who looks like she has killed before and would kill again

The 15-year-old girl who is ONLY 15 can you believe she is only 15!

The OAP with an obvious social disorder but it's fun to laugh at him

And they are all bloody awful!

I assume it's like Christmas but more extreme.

My life is a lot like the Dickens' novel A *Christmas Carol*, I spend an evening with three spirits and the next day I wake up and have to apologise to everyone I have ever met.

The Christmas season starts approximately just after Easter, when shops apparently forget how time works and need to throw tat at us. A Christmas-flavoured hummus, a Santa-scented bleach... anything they can slot into this holiday, they will. If anyone is still surprised about the commercialisation of Christmas then you have to wonder how they conduct themselves in day-to-day life without exploding every day. It's the biggest money grab of the year, and if companies controlled the calendar, it would be Christmas Day every other day.

But it is a magical time of year. We gather with our families for a week of elongated questioning – 'You've gained weight' when said with the vocal affliction of a question is still not a question. So you lie, you lie to the people you love the most. Instead of screaming AWFUL at someone you reply with 'fine, thanks' when asked how life is. You make your job sound 100 times more interesting than it actually is. You disguise yourself as a functioning member of society to impress people for a week so they don't see through the disguise and discover that all you've been doing all year is avoiding human contact and drinking.

There is one saving grace, though: day drinking. Christmas is one of the only two days of the year (your birthday being the other) when you are socially allowed to drink during the day without your family calling an intervention. It's the epitome of Western decadence: you wake up, you eat until you feel like a beach ball filled with gravy, and then you drink until you can't remember how much you've spent this holiday season.

WHAT YOUR CHRISTMAS PRESENTS REALLY MEAN

SOCKS
'You are a boring person and we couldn't figure out what to get you so have some socks.'

CHRISTMAS THEMED FOOD
'Here is a present that will become pointless as of Boxing Day. Also, you look like you like to eat so here's some more.'

PERFUME OR TOILETRIES
'You smell like complete shit and don't seem to be taking care of this yourself so here is a less than subtle hint.'

BOOKS
'Please, for the love of God, read something. It's like talking to a laundry basket trying to hold a conversation with you.'

A SCENTED CANDLE
'You are a woman between the ages of 18–80 with loads of random crap around your house so here is a fucking candle for some reason.'

AND OTHER TEXT SPEAK

Language for people who send dick pics.

Do you emoji? Do you and your partner finish text messages with an impractical amount of x's? Then you sicken me.

At some point in the near future we will all be writing solely in EMOJIS, reverting back to the time of the Egyptians and hieroglyphs. As I stated in the cats section, we are already turning back to this way of life, now we just need to start burying people in massive triangles.

Most digital language is a LIE. People who say 'LOL' type it with a face of complete apathy. Those who claim to roll around on the floor laughing have probably never laughed in their entire lives. A friend on MSN Messenger told me he would BRB. That was 12 years ago, I have not forgotten.

If you ever need a laugh, simply tell an elderly relative that LOL means lots of love, then see brilliant Facebook comments such as 'So sorry Graham is ill LOL' or 'I can't believe it, he was so young. LOL'.

Abbreviations are a natural evolution of language... 'Hello', got shortened to hi, and before 'hello', it was hellographicomorning. But Internet language when transferred to the real world is an embarrassing and painful experience. When you hear someone say 'lol' in real life a part of you dies, like a Horcrux that's been broken. One of the worst things that can happen to anyone, worse than your parents finding your internet history, is accidentally putting an 'x' on the end of an email to your boss. That shit will haunt you for years.

KNOW YOUR INTERNET SLANG

What are your kids really saying online?

lol – 'Lots of legs'
LMAO – 'Lost my artichokes, Mabel' - Code for drugs
ROFL – 'Rolf is near' – There are paedos about
imo – 'In my orifices'
ICYMI – 'In case Yugoslavia make it'
B4 – 'THERE ARE 4 BEES IN THIS ROOM'
ASAP – 'Anal sex after playtime'
YOLO – 'You organise laundry, OK'
Bae – 'A common misspelling of BEES'
smh – 'Sexy muppet handjob'
TL;DR – 'Twenty Lapdances at the Dirty Rodeo'
IRL – 'Internal rectal leakage'
FYI – 'FIRE. YOU IDIOT'
BTW – 'Bag that whale'
BFF – 'Best French fancy'
WTF – 'Where are The Females?'
ROFLCOPTER – 'A sort of transportation to Banterland'
BANTS – 'Like laughter, but for twats'

X-RAY

Looking inside that sweaty skin covered
sleeping bag you call your body.

The human body is a bizarre thing. I am not a doctor, but I did once tell a co-worker that 'the sniffles are going around at the moment' so I think that qualifies me to talk about human physiology. The body is essentially a super computer powering a exoskeleton made of steak around the place. Our entire being, our personalities and our faults are kept in what looks like a basketball made of afterbirth. Not a pleasant image, is it? Well, that's the human body for you. It's terribly unpleasant. We are all the same on the inside. There is no changing that. Some people have webbed toes and some people are Welsh, but on the inside we are all the same.

The heart runs the show, chucking bloody through four different rooms before launching it back through our body. Then you have your lungs, which look like two inflatable air beds filled with nicotine. The liver is the body's gutter, taking one for the team and filling itself with booze so the rest of the street can look nice. Kidneys are used for urine or something. I am not a doctor, do not quote any of this at a GP.

We treat our bodies terribly, apart from people who have disorders such as exercise or healthy living, but those people are a different story. We have to treat our bodies badly, how else will we know what we are allergic to? How else will we know what would kill us? My body is a temple, but a temple filled with chicken nuggets because an empty temple would be really boring.

~X

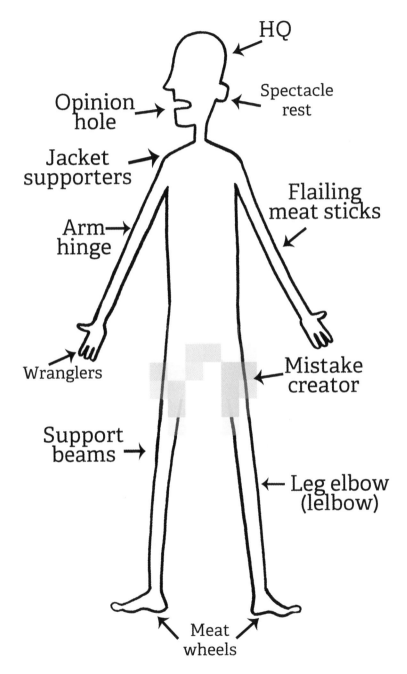

HQ

Spectacle
rest

Opinion
hole

Jacket
supporters

Flailing
meat sticks

Arm
hinge

Wranglers

Mistake
creator

Support
beams

Leg elbow
(lelbow)

Meat
wheels

YOGA

Human Tetris for people who eat kale.

In Matt Haig's book *Reasons to Stay Alive* he swears by yoga as a way to tackle depression. So, as an open-minded man (shut up), I gave this a go. As the relaxing music began, it became drowned out by my wife saying that smoking a cigarette and drinking rum was not what you were supposed to be doing in Downward Dog. Every position I moved into my bones cracked with dull thuds like a branch being snapped by a coconut crab. The woman on the video, whose body barely wobbled at all and looked like an Action Man doll, kept instructing us to keep going. That we could do this. To feel the burn. If I know one thing about my own physiology is that when I start feeling a burning sensation I should go to the doctor for 'that test'.

I have no problem with how people choose to abuse their own bodies: it is completely up to you. If your coke habit makes you happy, go for it. If your addiction to Sherlock fan fiction keeps you from going quite, quite mad then it's fine. Want to twist your body into a shape only sexually frustrated gibbons should make?

People find their inner Zen through various different and confusing ways. If these ways work for you, GREAT! All of your Facebook friends are SUPER HAPPY that you made a meal that looks like the jolly green giant threw up in an organic food shop. I find it calming to look at naked people on the internet, but is it OK when I post this to my timeline? With details, maps and statistics? No. I get pamphlets about finding Jesus sent to me from all my friends, while the sycophants who go jogging roam free.

The breezy
crotch

Ooh a penny

Arse
squats

Downward
dolphin

Upward
caterpillar

Diagonal
gibbon

Disaster

Human
semaphore

Stick your whole
foot up your
arse

YOU COME HERE OFTEN?

A subtler way of screaming 'I WANT TO DO THINGS TO YOU' at someone.

It is a fact, a solid FACT, that the greatest chat-up line ever is 'Hey, are you my big toe? Because I'm probably going to bang you on the coffee table later'. If that doesn't get you laid then you are a hideous human being with the personality of a heap of Zoo magazines and the face of a volleyball covered in kebab meat.

First impressions are important when attracting a mate. The superb Bird of Paradise (guessing the scientists had had one too many jungle mushrooms that day) attracts a mate by dancing at its mate while looking like a frisbee from *Tron*. This display is perfectly choreographed but often results in dismissal. Men, on the other hand – normal men – display a mating ritual similar to this, but not quite so beautiful. They apply their plumage in brightly coloured polo tops, then stagger over to their desired mate, and instead of a choreographed dance, they stumble about while shouting the words, 'CAN I DRINK YOU A BUY?' and falling over. This usually doesn't work.

There is one foolproof method to attract a mate with a chat-up line, so listen carefully. Like Neil Strauss says in his hetero novel of bullshit *The Game*, there is an art to picking up women. First, moonwalk into the bar. It doesn't matter if it's an English pub or a five-star steakhouse, moonwalk: you will get everyone's attention. As you sit at the bar and order a single shot of whisky, then shoot off the fireworks you have hidden in your jacket. Then loudly scream 'CONGA LINE!' and begin the Conga around the bar. Once you are covered in women, bring out your book of pictures of puppies and tell them the story about how your puppy is at home with a broken leg. DONE! You're welcome.

For women, these are the tips you need to remember to get a man to fall in love with you:

1. Stock the fridge with his favourite drinks. Then start drinking his favourite drinks. Become his favourite drinks. Burp at him if he complains.

2. Fill his underwear drawer with bees to teach him about blindly trusting people.

3. If he asks you to make him a sandwich, use your powers to summon a demon from the netherworld to transform him into a BLT.

4. Email him during his work day with Game Of Thrones spoilers. This will remind him that he can't read.

5. Answer the door to him naked, or better yet, without your skin in your true form of NIGHTSCAR THE DIMENSION SHIFTER

6. Let him fix small things around the house. Like microwaves or his issues with his distant parents.

7. Show you know about his favourite sport team by supporting their rivals and decorating your house in that colour.

8. Treat his friends the way you treat your own, so don't talk to them because Sarah can fuck off after what she did at the weekend.

9. Sit side by side when watching TV, Sit on him whilst watching TV. Sit in a different house whilst watching TV

10. Sell his organs during the night to show your dominance.

HOW TO ATTRACT A COPULATION BUDDY

Chat-up lines are all well and good, but you need to know how not to be a complete cunt.

STEP 1
Be nice, you twat! Neil Strauss and his ideas can get in the fucking bin! Nobody wants an arrogant moron.

STEP 2
Talk about the other person. Not yourself, you hear about yourself all the time. Fucking boring, isn't it? What do they do? Are they a fisherman? A competitive eater? Find out!

STEP 3
Don't just try and get really drunk. All that will happen is that you will think you've just told the best joke of all time and what you actually said was 'AIJSHGIAUHDGIHJDSAKGJNS'.

STEP 4
Release the 24 doves you have been keeping in your clothing all night. Release them in an entirely inappropriate fashion. NOW. DO IT NOW.

STEP 5
You're welcome.

YOUTH

A way to criticise young people for doing everything wrong. Ever.

Teenagers, the scourge of humanity. With their selfies and their Snapchats and their talky pictures, they'll never understand what it was REALLY like to be teenagers. Back in my day we listened to PROPER music, with PROPER lyrics, like 'I'm blue daba dee daba da'. We had proper haircuts, and we only engaged in carnal relations after a jury of our peers had allowed it.

Any sentences resembling those in the paragraph above can simply be replaced with 'Fucking hell, I wish I was a teenager!' Being a teenager is fucking brilliant. You are supposed to mess up, you are expected to ruin everything at least twice, you make LOADS of mistakes and never EVER learn a lesson. You go through phases which make no sense whatsoever. For instance, for a brief six-month period in 2004 I was an overweight Goth who enjoyed the music of Limp Bizkit. (Don't do drugs, kids.)

Being a teenager in any generation is rough. People older than you just want you to think about the future, to figure out how you want to sell your labour and to pay tax until you DIE. My favourite complaint about the youth of today is 'Oh, these kids are always on their smartphones'. Well, yes, my smartphone holds the entirety of human knowledge, the thoughts and feelings of millions of people of a similar age. I can watch an opera with a single press, I can research blogs regarding my sexuality without an awkward conversation with a reluctant parent, so I am sorry if I don't want to hear about Uncle Peter's foot disease over dinner.

Why the youth are LUCKY and never have to worry about ANYTHING

 They never have to worry about decorating a house because they will never be able to afford one.

They never have to worry about getting to work late because they will never be able to get a job.

They can be single forever because families are really expensive and one-night stands are more fun than families.

 They can stay fit and healthy as they have to walk everywhere because cars are only for rich people and drug dealers.

The youth of today don't know how good they have it.

YouTube

Like watching You've Been Framed
but without the internal bleeding.

You haven't lived until you're six hours into a video titled 'Goat screaming on repeat for 10 hours' and realise you are having a nervous breakdown. Or you're on the 130th episode of *The insanity of Ronald McDonald* at 7am after not sleeping for two days and realise you are wasting your life.

In times gone by people used to have to take lessons in how to change a bulb, fix a toaster or apply lipstick. Now we can simply watch an annoyingly smug person tell us how to do it FOR FREE. If you can tolerate the voice of a 13-year-old talking about photoshop, butt plugs or French, you can quite literally learn anything from free tutorials that you can access from your phone.

As with everything today, capitalism has COMPLETELY RUINED IT. If you want to watch a car advert on YouTube, you have to sit through a car advert you DIDN'T want to see. Videos now have more annoying text boxes over them than a 3am Japanese game show. And if it couldn't get any worse, young people are making money off it. Professional YouTubers are now a thing, giving birth to a new generation of Nick Grimshaws and Alex Zanes; it's like a post-apocalyptic nightmare where everything is controlled by T4 presenters.

Most of the shows YouTubers create are 15-minute-long adverts, from a chap screaming at video games to young women giggling into their foundation brushes. People who can't afford anything sit in their houses watching other people talk about how they can afford things. It's like watching a John Hughes' movie set in a Debenhams while on MDMA.

Warning:
You are unable to watch this video because it looks fucking awful. Seriously. It's just some American guy with his top off talking about video games or something. Please, go do something else. Watch a video of a panda on a slide or something.

LOL x360noscopex REAL footage OMG

Uploaded by SwagCaptain69

Best of YouTube

#Music

Looking for your favourite music video? Well, we have thousands of covers, the song just ripped from a CD with no video and teenagers covering it with a banjo or a keyboard or some shit. What you want is only a few thousand annoying clicks away!

PREVIEW

#PopularOnYouTubeUnitedKingdom

The videos that are currently popular in your country will make you despair for the state of your country! Are you out of touch, or are the kids wrong? Find out! Click this playlist to find lots of annoying youngsters who look like topshop threw up on a secondary school student, up-and-coming musicians who sound like ducks screaming into a pillow, and video blogs of people talking about shit you don't care about!

#Gaming

Love gaming? Love watching people playing video games? Well, tough shit, all we have is people screaming over video game footage and finding themselves hilarious! Enjoy.

PREVIEW

Movies

All of your favourite trailers and scenes from movies, handily hidden in a maze of reviews, dubbed versions and parodies! Want to see that scene from Reservoir Dogs where he cuts the dude's ear off? Well, we don't have that due to copyright issues but there's a video of dogs doing it! Want to see your favourite movie trailers? Well, too bad! All the trailers have an american teenager giving you their opinion over them! It's like your mate who talks all the way through movies and won't shut up but worse!

ZED

Frankly, a stupid fucking letter.

OK, I'll be honest with you here, when the publishing company suggested an A – Z format for this book I was OVER THE MOON. However, upon getting to Z, and trying to think of subjects that can relate to modern-day life, I fell short. I slipped into a cavern of writing despair, wondering how I could write a chapter on Zod from *Superman* and how I could tie it to George Osborne. So the Z's in this book are TENUOUS links at best. Anyway, back to your regularly scheduled programme.

~Z

IDEAS FOR Z

- ~~ZEBRAS~~ - WHY ZEBRAS CAN SHI~
  ARE ZEBRAS RACIST HOR~

- ZIMBABWE - JUST PICTURES OF MUG~
  LOOKING AT THINGS?

- X ZOOPHILLIA - NO. LET'S NOT GO THER~

- ZIPS X - WHAT THE FUCK AM I DOING

- WHAT? ZOOEY DESCHANEL'S ANNOYING QUIRKY
  BOLLOCKS?

- X ZINC - ..... NOT A CLUE

- X ZEPHYR - RED HOT CHILLI PEPPERS CAN
  GET IN THE FUCKING BIN

- ZOMBIES X - CAN ZOMBIES LOVE? CAN THEY?!

- ZYGOTE X - STOP NOW AARON

- ZONE X - WHAT

- ZIRCONIA X - FUCKS SAKE WHAT AM I

- MORE X ZEBRAS - DOING WITH MY LIFE

ZIG ZAGGING

And other stupid Hollywood Tropes.
Like aliens, or friendship.

Hollywood gives us a lot of greatly exaggerated scenarios with very little grounding in the real world. We are supposed to learn from cinema, to better ourselves and relate to the characters onscreen. To learn life lessons and to expand our knowledge. Instead we get told that refrigerators can protect you from nuclear detonations and that Channing Tatum is not supposed to look like an Easter Island head on a wheel of cheese.

Unrealistic movie expectations are everywhere. I have been mugged, yet during the mugging the perpetrator did start telling me his masterplan – how he would use my credit cards and phone – talking away to give me ample time to escape. In action flicks, the protagonist almost always gets shot in the leg or shoulder, but just carries on running about the place like Mo Farah on ketamine. I once got shot in the leg with a paintball and I never wanted to ever move again. Know that bit towards the end of the second act in a Rom-Com, the couple who we're supposed to be cheering for have an argument and it looks like it may not work out? Even though there are 40 minutes

HOW TO UNDERSTAND TACTICAL SIGN LANGUAGE IN ACTION FLICKS:

to go? In real life you don't get this. Ever tried running alongside a train to shout 'I LOVE YOU' to someone? One, trains are really fucking loud so you can't be heard. And two, most trains go faster than the average person. Ever tried to run through airport security to stop your loved one getting on a plane? No, of course you haven't because security would chase you down, beat the shit out of you, then lock you in a grey room for a week while they charge you with terrorism.

Yes it's all make-believe, but you have to ground some of it in realism. I can't accept that a woman can outrun a T-Rex while wearing heels, or that the first Death Star wasn't insured. It's just too far-fetched. A realistic Hollywood blockbuster would look something like this:

"So, these giant anthrax moths are threatening to destroy the United States"

"My God"

"Jim, you're on your last day until retirement, your wife is an unlikeable side character and we never actually see your kid, you just elude to his existence. Want to battle the giant anthrax moths?"

"Yes"

"Marvellous, now if you could fill out these insurance forms protecting the company from your inevitable injuries and whatever public property you will destroy in the two set pieces towards the end of this movie that would be, ok never mind, while you were filling in the forms the anthrax moth destroyed the world. God dammit Jim. You fuck."

ZOOLOGY

The science of Zoos. I think.

Animals are fucking stupid. Very few of them have a knowledge of economics, none of them vote and many of them can't even pass the first level on Candy Crush. So as punishment for them not contributing to society we tend to put them in Animal Jail. Whales and dolphins get put in 'Sea World', a Guantánamo for fish. Anything that can bimble around on land we shove into boxes so we can laugh at them through glass.

There are a few exceptions. We turn some animals into modern-day court jesters, keeping them around for our own amusement. We allow cats and dogs and snakes and massive spiders to live in our house, sleep in our beds, because we trust them. Little do we know that one day, when the animal rebellion begins, and we are forced into zoos, and we spend our days being gawked at by fat American gophers that we will have to accept our fate.

We can all agree that animals are better than humans. They have no concept of Michael Bay films. They know nothing of the TV Jeremy Clarkson has forced into existence. In many ways they have got their lives sorted. People who say that animals are more afraid of us than we are of them have never been in the room while a cat is having a shit fit. They've obviously never been mercilessly attacked by a wasp the size of a caravan. Animals have developed ways to shit people up. They will poison us, attack us and eat us if they get the chance. That squirrel outside your house right now? He probably has a gun. And when he learns how to use it, we are all going to pay for our disrespect.

Tiny eyes where a soul used to be

Shite mohawk

Beak used for picking at dead children

Wings for no fucking reason

Tummy is a sled

Legs that look like an old man's scrotum

PENGUIN FACTS

Penguins don't pay Tax

They vomit on their children

Can't drive

Refuse to speak English

Can't work or WON'T WORK?

Bastards

ZEITGEIST

The End.

OK, yes, Zeitgeist is an awful word to finish on, but it's the only synonym for THE END that I could find on Google that started with Z. I hope reading this hasn't been an ordeal for you. I hope the internal bleeding was minimal and any loss of IQ that may have occurred was completely coincidental. I hope these 104 little rants didn't make you want to set your family on fire and turn to religion.

This brief little sign-off is to say thank you. Thank you for reading this package of nonsense, this pessimistic view of our current state of being. I am not one for answers, yet I am not one for leaving something unfinished. All the problems in this book can be solved or at least rectified with a little help. We are that help, our voices a chorus of opinion that must be heard. If you are not happy with something, shout about it; if you are hurting, then write about it. Obviously, if you are hurting physically and need medical attention, the writing can wait.

All I know is that without you guys, the people who follow me on Twitter and those who are reading this book, I wouldn't be who I am now. Thank you for letting me annoy you with my presence, because no matter how insignificant or minuscule my stupid words are to you, the fact that you have read them makes everything worth it. Your hair looks nice again today, by the way.